The Parables Of Jesus And Their Flip Side

Cycles A, B, and C

*Parables of Jesus
from the Revised Common Lectionary
with a fresh look at the other side of the story*

Jerry L. Schmalenberger

CSS Publishing Company, Inc., Lima, Ohio

THE PARABLES OF JESUS AND THEIR FLIP SIDE

Copyright © 2001 by
CSS Publishing Company, Inc.
Lima, Ohio

Library of Congress Cataloging-in-Publication Data

Schmalenberger, Jerry L.
    The parables of Jesus and their flip side : cycles A, B, and C / Jerry L. Schmalenberger.
       p. cm.
    "Parables of Jesus from the Revised common lectionary with a fresh look at the other side of the story."
    ISBN 0-7880-1816-7 (alk. paper)
    1. Jesus Christ—Parables—Homiletical use. 2. Jesus Christ—Parables—Sermons. Sermons, American. I. Title.
BT375.2 .S33 2001
252'.6—dc21
                                      2001025082
                                          CIP

ISBN 0-7880-1816-7

*This book of sermons based on Jesus' parables
is dedicated to that little band of disciples
who gather at Pacific Lutheran Theological Seminary
annually to better prepare that "seed bed" for ministry.
It was from them I first gained encouragement
for my "flip side theology."*

Table Of Contents

Foreword   7

Preface   9

Introduction   11

Cycle A

Proper 4   **Rebuilding On**   13
Pentecost 2   **Secure Foundations**
Ordinary Time 9   *Matthew 7:21-29*

Proper 10   **A Story For**   19
Pentecost 8   **The Discouraged**
Ordinary Time 15   *Matthew 13:1-9, 18-23*

Proper 12   **Small Beginnings Which**   25
Pentecost 10   **Produce Large Results**
Ordinary Time 17   *Matthew 13:31-33, 44*

Proper 20   **Grace Isn't Fair**   33
Pentecost 18   *Matthew 20:1-16*
Ordinary Time 25

Proper 22   **Some Tenants Are Better**   39
Pentecost 20   **Than Other Tenants**
Ordinary Time 27   *Matthew 21:33-46*

Proper 23   **Joy, Grace, And**   45
Pentecost 21   **Living Together**
Ordinary Time 28   *Matthew 22:1-14*

Proper 28   **In Celebration Of**   51
Pentecost 26   **The One-Talent Person**
Ordinary Time 33   *Matthew 25:14-30*

Cycle B

Proper 6
Pentecost 4
Ordinary Time 11

(See Proper 12, Cycle A
  parallel text)
Mark 4:26-34

25

Cycle C

Proper 10
Pentecost 8
Ordinary Time 15

**Safer Roads
  And Real Life**
Luke 10:25-37

57

Proper 19
Pentecost 17
Ordinary Time 24

**The Never Lost
  Ninety-Nine**
Luke 15:1-10

63

Lent 4

**Love That Just
  Won't Quit**
Luke 15:1-3, 11-32

69

Proper 21
Pentecost 19
Ordinary Time 26

**Dog-Licked Sores
  And Linen Underwear**
Luke 16:19-31

75

Proper 25
Pentecost 23
Ordinary Time 30

**Going Home
  Justified**
Luke 18:9-14

81

*I will open my mouth in parables, I will
utter hidden things, things from old.*
— Psalm 78:2

Foreword

There are two sides of the stone on the way: one side which we can see and on which we walk — and the other side underneath which is hidden and rather dark. Probably this metaphor is a principle of being in this world at all. For there are always two sides within human life: the appearance, the manifestation, the daylight on the one side and the darkness of things, the mystery of life, the "otherness" of reality on the other side. But please take the chance and turn the stone over, and you will find there a world full of wonders: creative ground and tiny creations, slender roots, and the tender veining of the stone itself. Looking at the other side of reality means finally deepening all those detections and fundamentally widening the world in its depths as well.

Jerry Schmalenberger, former President and Professor of Parish Ministry at the Pacific Lutheran Seminary in Berkeley, California, has developed exactly this concept by using a metaphor of modern time for his approach to understand biblical texts in an up-to-date way. He calls this concept and — even more — this vision a *Flip Side Theology*.

Jerry Schmalenberger, an outstanding preacher and well known teacher of Homiletics, puts it in these words: "In my younger days before the advent of CDs, music records all had a flip side. The popular tune was on one side of the '78' or '45,' or later the '33-1/3,' but if you turned it over you would find less familiar melodies. Once in a while one of these flip side tunes would hit it big ...

"Long ago I sensed a flip side to my teaching in my ministry. I got a lot more out of it than those who came to learn. I was more and more certain of this flip side of teaching as my own confidence and knowledge about the scripture, symbols, and faith grew because of my teaching ... I have concluded this flip side of preaching is nearly as important as the popular side of what the preaching event does for those who hear."

Indeed, this unusual theory is not just a new kind of homiletical technique. It is much more, probably a kind of a new hermeneutical paradigm: looking not only at the manifestation or the main

7

characteristics of the message, but also "turning over the stone" and detecting the "otherness" of this text with its new and surprising tunes, the depth of its symbols, the longing of its figures for peace and salvation.

Truly, this "Flip Side Theology" is important: important for approaching biblical texts of all kinds and especially important for approaching the parables which we find in the Gospels. For the parables are, so-to-speak, of a bi-polar structure. On the one side there is the "imagery," the dimension of metaphors and symbols, ideas and stories. On the other side there is the "reality," the realm of concrete life at which the literary form of the parable is pointing. Actually there is a special relationship between the "Flip Side Theology" and the literary genus or kind of the parables, and you might decide by yourself which one the flip side really is: the "imagery" or the "reality."

After all the "Flip Side Theology," as Jerry Schmalenberger has formulated it, is a very interesting and very inspiring approach to biblical texts and to Christian traditions as well. I do wish that this new and unique way of looking at the hidden agendas and of listening to its hidden tunes will be well received by attentive readers and listeners, and last, but not least, I do wish God's blessing for this outstanding book and for its author on his way.

Professor Dr. Richard Riess
Augustana Hochschule,
Neuendettelsau, Bavaria, Germany

Preface

I prepared this volume of sermons in the pleasant little Franconian town of Neuendettelsau, Germany. There, while lecturing at the Bavarian Augustana Hochschule, I developed what I like to call flip-side theology. In the shadow of the great nineteenth century preacher, Wilhelm Loehe, who called this place his quiet wilderness, came the inspiration for these sermons.

The books which I often consulted were: *The Gospel According to Matthew*, by A.W. Argyle, Cambridge, at the University Press, 1963; *The Interpreter's One-Volume Commentary on the Bible*, Abingdon Press, Nashville, 1971; *The Daily Study Bible*, Matthew and Luke, by William Barclay, Westminster Press, Philadelphia, 1958; *Stepping Stones of the Steward,* by Ronald E. Vallet, William B. Eerdmans Publishing Company, Grand Rapids, Michigan, 1989; *The Moffatt New Testament Commentary*, The Gospel of Luke, by Wm. Manson, Hodder and Stoughton, London, 1963; *The Gospel According to Luke*, commentary by E.J. Tinsley, Cambridge, at the University Press, 1969; *How to Preach a Parable,* by Eugene L. Lowry, Abingdon Press, Nashville, 1989.

The series began as a brief set of nightly devotions on parables and miracles given to our work/study groups which meet each August at Pacific Lutheran Theological Seminary. It was their gentle encouragement which motivated me to write.

Thanks to Carol Schmalenberger for all the editing and Dorothy A. Lindstrom for reading and putting my hand-written manuscript into computer format with editing.

Two of my colleagues on the Augustana Hochschule faculty have been very helpful and encouraging: Rektor and New Testament scholar Wolfgang Stegemann and Homiletitian Richard Riess are in my gratitude.

And, as always is the case, thanks for the fine cooperation and support from CSS Publishing which has played such a big part in my ministry and life.

Jerry L. Schmalenberger

Introduction

Italian scholar Umbarto Eco uses the Latin phrase *Lector in Fabula* to say that the reader of the miracles and parables of Jesus is in the story as well.

This is the second volume of sermons which deal not only with the primary focus of the story but also turn the narrative upside down to see what might be learned from a different perspective. The companion volume is called *The Miracles Of Jesus And Their Flip Side* (CSS), 2000. Just like musical records used to have a primary side on which one played the popular and familiar tunes and a "flip side" on which were the less known tunes, so we have examined the flip side of the parables. As Eco claims, the reader becomes a part of the story as well as the very familiar shepherds, widows, Pharisees, lost son, and so on.

In composing these homiletical messages I like the following moves in the story plot:

1. Run the story (in traditional or contemporary form).
2. Tell what it teaches about God.
3. Explain what it reveals about us.
4. Consider why the author wrote it down.
5. Look for a fresh flip side.
6. Answer the "so what?"
7. Frame it by returning to the beginning.

Notice I have placed the above numbers in the eleventh sermon titled, "Dog-Licked Sores And Linen Underwear," so you can easily discern the moves.

Down through the centuries we preachers have been admonished not to treat the story (parable) as allegory, giving each person or element a special meaning. However, it seems to me it is legitimate to see if there might be on the other side of the main focus an important message for our day and culture, which makes the gospel as relevant or perhaps even more relevant than the historical interpretation.

11

This flip side theology might be carried out even further when we make the claim that preaching may be mostly for the preacher, witnessing for the person who witnesses, care giving for the one who gives the loving care, and financial stewardship for the one who gives the money away. But that's the subject for yet another writing while the fingers and mind are nimble enough to do it.

— JLS

Rebuilding On
Secure Foundations

Matthew 7:21-29; Genesis 6:11ff

I live in Northern California where we frequently experience earthquakes and mud slides. We know the consequences of a shabby foundation. When the earth shakes, the house vibrates right off its moorings, often collapsing in a heap. Sometimes things not fastened down, like a water heater, will break its gas line and a disastrous fire starts.

Then there are the rains of winter when whole hillsides give way and envelop those below in a heavy, invading mud. Often houses built on the top of sandy hills, where Californians seem to like to build, slowly come sliding down the hill only to end up as a pile of rubbish below.

Our parable of Jesus tells of similar circumstances. Carpenter Jesus knew well the results of poor foundations. No doubt he had seen the contrast when what had been dry, pleasant, summer stream beds became raging torrents in the winter. He had seen with his own eyes the lazy man's way of building. In order not to have to carry heavy boulders up the hill and not to have to dig down to the solid rock for foundation, they built on the flimsy, soft sand of the valleys called "wadis."

In fact, Matthew tells the story of the builders constructing the house in two different locations: one sandy, one on rock; Luke says it was the same location with one built on top but the other dug down to rock. Either way, the traditional teaching is the same.

We need good foundations for rough weather when it comes. And it does come into all our lives. We live in a very imperfect world with other imperfect people. And often how and where we live is in accordance to the principles and laws of nature.

So some of the storms for which we need a strong foundation might be that sudden terminal illness is discovered in us or our loved ones, or

- when one of our children bitterly disappoints us with his or her behavior;
- when a spouse is unfaithful;
- when we lose our job or status;
- when a friend circumvents our relationship;
- when a neighbor disgraces the neighborhood;
- when someone lets us down whom we had been counting on; or
- when a significant other walks out without warning.

We need a solid, rock-grounded foundation to hang onto to survive the threatening storm when the floods of winter come. Like sheer walls for earthquake protection in California where I live, we need something which doesn't give way when our lives are shaken right down to the very foundation.

Out here in earthquake and mudslide country, one thing which is essential for our security is to bolt the side walls to the foundation. This is something which has been omitted in years gone by. Now the building codes require it. Those life-securing bolts for a dependable foundation might be such as:

- a faithful prayer life which keeps us in tune with God's will for us;
- regular worship here in church where others can help us foundation build;
- continued growing in our knowledge of Christ and his word;
- close fellowship with others who have weathered the storms of life well;
- lifestyle priorities which are based on other's needs rather than on our own gratification and happiness;
- a ministry we carry out in our daily lives where we live, work, and play.

Of course we can't avoid some of life's worst and most violent storms, but for the most part what we can do is prepare ourselves for the bad weather and learn the ways to get through.

14

I once saw the heavy trailer, of a tractor-trailer combination, parked on an asphalt parking lot. Those metal wheels which crank down to free it from the tractor were sinking deeper and deeper into the asphalt and may have already gone all the way through. The driver had thought it looked like a solid foundation on which to park the trailer — but not so. There are many such thin foundations into which we will sink. Check your foundation.

I believe the reason Jesus put this story about weak foundations in his teaching is expressed in verse 24: "Therefore everyone who hears these words of mine and *puts them into practice* is like a wise man...."

It's an idea that's just beginning to mature in my own beliefs about God. Doing what one hears is the way we really come to own and believe what we have been taught.

Let's take this to a radical conclusion: the one who witnesses to someone else much better believes what he has said. The preacher who preaches the gospel better owns that gospel. The teacher who instructs others on discipleship better understands the call by Jesus to be a disciple. The Christian who actually prays for his or her enemies knows the wisdom in that admonition. So does the one who actually turns the other cheek.

James understood this when he wrote, "Do not merely listen to the word, and so deceive yourselves. Do what it says ... not forgetting what you have heard, but doing it — he will be blessed in what he does" (James 1:22-23).

And Paul understood it also. He wrote to the church in Rome, "For it is not those who hear the law who are righteous in God's sight, but it is those who *obey* the law who will be declared righteous" (Romans 2:13).

So it is by doing, as well as hearing, that we "batten down the hatches" for life's inevitable storms.

In order to understand Jesus' teaching to be kind to each other, we must go out and be kind. As we do this, we'll have a much deeper meaning of it. In order to comprehend Jesus' teaching of going the extra mile, we must start on that second mile this week. We'll understand as never before.

Many years ago preachers retold this parable as a warning about the judgment and as preparation for eternal life. They claimed we needed to get ourselves ready for the return of Jesus and the decisions about ourselves and lives beyond the grave.

I'm not sure that ever was the main reason for the story. After all, this was told *before* the sacrifice of our Savior on the cross and his resurrection from the Easter tomb. It was *before* he returned in Spirit on Pentecost to be with us now.

So our fate in judgment is not dependent on the retrofitting of our foundations by hearing the law and keeping it. It is our acceptance of the grace-gift of salvation accomplished for us by the one who was telling the parable in the first place.

Now the good foundation is baptism and faith in a Savior who wants to see us through all kinds of weather right into eternal life with him. Our foundation is the rock of Christ and it is secure. We just ought live like it as a grateful response.

Perhaps a weak foundation built on sand in our day should be those who judge the church of Jesus Christ without hearing it. It seems like our culture and times are full of people who ignore or ridicule the church without really knowing it. They have heard some televangelist or have seen a television or movie portrayal of clergy or church and based their opinion about the lack of relevance on that.

There are many who believe you have to leave your brains at the door to be a believer. There are many who believe Christianity is for the feminine or the weak or only the misfits of society. They have decided, without really hearing. Jesus claims here, "... everyone who *hears* these words of mine ... is like a wise person ..." (Matthew 8:24).

There is another side to this parable — let's call it the flip side. As a record or tape has one side on which the popular tunes are cut and on the other side are the more minor and less well-known melodies, so perhaps are the parables of Jesus. Examining the flip sides gives us a fresh interpretation and yet another teaching for discipleship. Sometimes they pack a punch even stronger than the first side!

16

For this one, the other side of the story may be that we almost always place ourselves as the wise person with the strong foundation. But are we? Perhaps not.

We are better described as the foolish whose house most often comes tumbling down from life's storms. Our situation is better described as one of *those who need to rebuild.* The storms come, the water rises, and down comes our houses which we thought were so secure.

There are many ways we can rebuild after one of our life's disasters. It's times like that when the congregation ought to surround, comfort, give encouragement to get us back on our feet again. There are always some of us who are in need of help with rebuilding. We can do that by praying for each other. We can do that by offering God's love at a time we may feel very unloved. We can do that by standing close to the one who has suffered loss. It doesn't always require profound words or great financial contributions. It just calls for our presence through which God's Holy Spirit comforts, guides, and brings healing.

Rebuilding after the loss suffered in the storm of life is grief-filled and painful. But we ought not have to ever do it alone. In fact, again and again we can rebuild even though again and again life tears us down — the foundation, our Christ, remains firm.

There is something else here. I wonder if while this foolish builder was not digging down to a solid rock foundation or just building in a sandy summertime "wadi," did anyone warn him of his mistake? Should not someone have intervened? Wasn't there a family member or friend who could have warned him?

This also is our task as disciples. We who know the instability of the river bed ought to share that information with those who do not know it. We must find a way to convince them to change the location to higher, more solid ground:
— to one addicted to wealth;
— to the person basing life on what can be accumulated;
— to those who are going deeper and deeper into drugs or alcohol;
— to those who trample on others to get power.

Let our lives as lived here be a warning sign to such as these: "Don't build here, ask me for another site."

The utility companies will come to mark your yard for location of electric, phone, and cable lines with their little red and yellow flags or paint from a spray can *before* you dig down to build or plant, so we must mark out the dangers for others who are preparing to build.

— Son, it is very dangerous to have unprotected sex.
— Daughter, be careful building your life on good looks alone.
— Brother, beware the perversion of your personality by giving in to racial hatred.
— Mother, it doesn't work to buy friendship.

Greed will devour you, jealousy will distort and spoil.

I remember at one of the Indy 500 races, a driver came in for a pit stop and crashed into his own pit crew. Someone had moved the red flags which mark where the driver should start putting on the brakes. We live in a time when the flags have all been moved and sometimes have been removed altogether. We need to mark again where the brakes need be applied. It's the same place where the builder must be careful about building.

This calls for a whole network of support groups in our congregation which will advise and counsel each other about building lives. It means, more importantly, help for rebuilding after the storms we all face from time to tragic time.

While in Amsterdam, I noticed how crooked many of the homes (especially around canals) are. They are braced with large logs up the front of the building. Perhaps that's the best image of how our building goes. We do have the Christ to support our flimsy structures.

For us who live in California with earthquakes and mud slides, it's an all too real parable. We know the value of sheer walls, plates bolted to foundations, and cross-the-wall studs support. And hopefully we know also the value of *warning* others about the sand, having *help* with rebuilding, *doing* as well as hearing, and *preparing* for the floods which do come.

A Story For
The Discouraged

Matthew 13:1-9, 18-23

The response was terrific! I can almost see some of the disciples like Peter, James, and John jumping up and down in excitement. There were crowds and crowds of people. Some were not there to learn but were rather curious about this wonder worker.

They pushed Jesus right out to the water's edge until he had to get in a boat and speak from it. Water does make for wonderful amplification of one's voice. He, seeing a farmer sowing some seed, used that scene to illustrate an important lesson for the crowd and the enthusiastic disciples.

The farmer carrying a bag of seed over one shoulder was reaching in with the other hand and in rhythm with his step, casting the precious seed on the ground. The point Jesus probably wanted most to get across that day was that our results will not all be the same when we try to plant the word of God in other people's lives. That's a great message for us when we get discouraged.

Later, the early church treated this parable as allegory which means they gave each part of the story a symbolic meaning: the shallow soil, hard soil, thistle-infested soil and, of course, the good, rich soil. I doubt Jesus had all that in mind.

Here is a wonderful story about expectation and discouragement. It says that people will each react differently to the same witness we give. One may be so angry and disappointed at a church or pastor, that he or she can't hear or believe the good news at all. Another may just hear because it's the fad at the moment and then abandon the whole thing later. Another may be doing so many good things in life, that the church and the Savior get completely crowded out.

But the nice part of this parable is the assurance that there always will be those who hear and believe, who grow and mature in their faith. This was a wonderful assurance for those disciples back there listening at water's edge and is a wonderful assurance to us who sometimes try so hard to witness but want to give up at the miserable results.

It was really an important message for that crowd and those disciples because at the time everything looked so good and successful. But the storm clouds were already gathering over Lake Galilee and before very long the crowd would melt away. Those who remained would turn hostile. A cross would be prepared in Jerusalem.

On days of discouragement like those ahead, the faithful would need to recall again and again this story of the farmer and his seed. And they did. Matthew, Mark, and Luke thought it so important that all three wrote it down.

A little later I want to stand this parable on its head and examine a whole different way of looking at it. But first, let's consider what it means to us personally today. I think there are times when we all are like the hard soil on the path next to the field.

— We get angry at the preacher.
— We get disappointed with the way things are done at the church.
— The national body makes announcements on controversial issues we just don't like.
— Changes are made which upset us.
— We pray for favors from God and it seems like God ignores us.

Sometimes we come to worship not expecting anything worthwhile to happen — and it doesn't. It's easy to let ourselves become closed and hard to the preaching and teaching, especially if it challenges us to think in new ways.

If you are in need of softening up the soil of your own soul, if so far your faith has been shallow, if in your life there are so many things which are crowding out learning and growing, then perhaps it's time to go into prayer for God's Spirit to help you change and be receptive to teaching, preaching, inspiration, and Christian guidance.

Becoming that good soil is possible, with God's help, for us. That's the good news here. We can move beyond lousy growing conditions to new, rich soil where we and our loved ones can mature in the faith.

Do you think, like a pastor giving a children's sermon which is really aiming for the adults listening, that Jesus may have been mainly aiming for his disciples? After Good Friday, Easter Sunday, Ascension, and the coming of God's Spirit on Pentecost, no doubt their preaching would be received in all the ways described in the parable. They would need this assurance that there would always be some good soil which would be fruitful.

But they would also need to be told by Jesus that there are dangers in discipleship. One can be hardened like that which must have happened to Judas. One can operate from shallow roots, going with every fad and impulse like big fisherman Peter. One can be influenced by outside considerations and have the primary focus crowded out like James and John when they began to worry about the "pecking order" in the kingdom.

This parable told by Jesus, with a boat for his pulpit, says: cultivate yourself, beware of getting sidetracked, be the rich soil you are intended to be.

In a book by J. Russell Hale, titled *Who are the Unchurched?* we learn the kinds of soil we may be in danger of becoming and the kinds of soil out there in which we are sent to sow the gospel.

— There are those who are *anti-institutionalist* who believe the church has become too preoccupied with its own self-interests.
— There are the *boxed-in* who have belonged but found membership in the church too confining.
— There are the many, many *burned out.* They feel the church has completely consumed their energy.
— There are the *happy hedonists* who devote their lives to pleasure-satisfying activities.
— Sadly, there are also those who consider themselves *locked out,* who feel the church has closed its doors to them.

21

— There is the largest group, according to Hale, whom he calls *the Publicans*. They have the preconceived idea that the church is primarily filled with Pharisees.
— In our day we must deal with the *scandalized* who think our disunity is a scandal which makes them reject us.
— There are not only the *true unbelievers*, but also the *pilgrims*, whose beliefs are in process of formation.

The list could go on but I think you see why we can expect all kinds of response to our witness. We can see also how easily we can have our own receptivity to the gospel harden, or scorch from the heat, or be choked out with thistles.

Please, dear God, cultivate me that I might be most of the time good soil.

There is an exciting flip side to this story Jesus told the crowd. We've seen the traditional way of interpreting the message. Let's consider a totally different approach: *perhaps the real message is not so much how we hear as how we sow.*

This is a parable not so much about soils as it is about how God sows and would have us sow. As Jesus looked up there on the hillside and saw a farmer broadcasting seed, he thought, "Look at how he throws those seeds in the most unpromising places. Everyone knows it doesn't stand a chance of growing there, but nevertheless, he still tries."

This really knocks down the idea we often use for not sharing the faith with someone else. We often rationalize away our opportunity to sow the seed of faith with words like these.
— They're not *our* people.
— No one would accept them in our congregation.
— They won't like our style of liturgical worship.
— They are too tough and turned off by the church to consider it now.
— They used to be members but got mad at the preacher.
— I asked them already and they said, "No."

The Old Testament scripture had it years before Jesus told this parable: "Sow your seed in the morning and at evening, let not your hands be idle, for you do not know which will succeed, whether this or that, or whether both will do equally well" (Ecclesiastes 11:6).

That hillside sower could have said that the right-of-way path was too hard for seed. Or that the shallow dirt-over-rock couldn't support plants. Or that the thistle would choke out good seed. But he planted anyway!

That's good news for us who are far from the deep, rich soil we should be. And it's good news for those we invite into the body of Christ for we will not give up on those either, no matter how hopeless and unpromising the situation may appear. We sow the seed and really leave the results to God. We sow the seed even though our first judgment is it isn't worth the effort.

But in response to the way the gospel was planted in us, as unproductive as it may have seemed, we do the same for others. And often God sees the possibilities when we just can't make them out. The difference is God's Spirit which helps us. When we sow seed by witnessing to someone else, we also can sow in the most unpromising places. The Spirit will take over and the response will surprise us because God is at work in our planting. And because we sow in such reckless ways and places, our own receptivity and understanding of the gospel reaps more and more harvest.

Here in the U.S., all active members of a Christian congregation usually know an average of six to eight unchurched friends, relatives, neighbors, or people they work with. They are, by far, the best soil in which we can sow our seed and expect the best results. Just think of the possibilities of the harvest here! A congregation which has 100 active members has from 600 to 800 unchurched people who are already inclined toward their church.

In church growth language this is called the *extended congregation*. They are people who live within driving distance of our building and who already have an acquaintance within the congregation whom they know fairly well. We must invite them. We know the seed is good and we know the ground is probably receptive. And even if it isn't, just like that Galilean farmer Jesus spotted from the moored fishing boat, we ought to try to plant regardless of its promise.

In the musical, *Evita*, Eva Peron said of herself: "I am content to be the woman who brought the people to Juan Peron." Perhaps we can be content to bring the gospel to people we know and care about.

At Our Primary Purpose, an alcoholic treatment center, Dick said, "I don't lecture; I just tell them how it was with me being drug-dependent." They understood and wanted that same help. Dick said to them, "I don't have to be alone anymore."

Our planting of the seed is like that. We just tell them about our relationship with God. We don't have to be alone anymore either.

So on the flip side of this parable we learn a lot about spreading the good news. No one is unpromising in God's sight. God would have us invite all — those of different skin color, those of different sexual orientation, those isolated by their wealth, those in prison, single, married, Republicans, Democrats, Green party and no party — the seed goes out and to God is left the results. Consider right now where you will sow this week.

From a simple fishing boat at the shore of Galilee's small lake comes a simple story with very big implications for us. It says God would have us sow everywhere. It also tells us not to be discouraged at the results. After all, the real kick is in the sowing.

Small Beginnings Which Produce Large Results

Matthew 13:31-33, 44

There is a small Franconian village in the rolling hills of Bavaria, Germany, which never ceases to amaze all who learn of its fantastic history.

In the mid-1800s, a young parish pastor came to this simple farming village named Neuendettelsau. Wilhelm Loehe is now known around the world for the work he was able to commence in his little "silent wilderness," as he called it. Pilgrims come yet today to visit from Brazil, the U.S., New Guinea, and other distant lands.

Considered by some as one of the finest preachers of the nineteenth century, Loehe understood the possibilities of beginning small, setting loose the power of God's kingdom in his little Franconian village. Whole families relocated from across Germany to be in his church and hear his kingdom-centered preaching.

Over one thousand missionaries have gone out from Neuendettelsau to distant countries of the world. A deaconess movement began that produced thousands of white-capped angels of mercy. Homes were built in the little village, now with 7,000 people, for orphans, ill, emotionally disturbed, physically handicapped, and the elderly. A Lutheran seminary was established as well. It's now called the Augustana Hochschule.

All this began in a very small way in a tiny village by a preacher who had been dismissed from his first two internships — but who knew the gospel's promise of tremendous possibilities from small beginnings.

25

Although he himself never visited here in the United States, Loehe and his disciples of Neuendettelsau are the founders of the Missouri Synod (along with C.W.F. Walther). They started seminaries in Fort Wayne, Indiana; Dubuque, Iowa; and my alma mater, Trinity Seminary in Columbus, Ohio. Missions to Native Americans were begun in Michigan and a whole synod developed in Iowa.

Jesus promised his followers it could be like that in the kingdom of God. Small beginnings, with some leaven of faith and those willing to sacrifice and pay a price, will produce amazing results.

The Gospel writer Matthew often arranged Jesus' teachings by similar subjects. That's what we are looking at in his thirteenth chapter. Jesus told of a mustard seed which is quite small and yet grows into a great tree. Then he told about what he had seen his mother often do — put a little lump of yeast in the bread dough and soon it would influence the whole of the flour. Next comes the story of Jesus using a simple metaphor of a treasure hidden in a field and how a man spent a lot to get that treasure by buying the field.

Put together, or taken individually, these stories teach a great lesson to us disciples who so often count the cost, the possibilities of failure, the meager size of the project compared with the problems to be addressed, and we never get started in the first place. But Jesus said — don't underestimate how a little beginning can grow and grow into spectacular results.

When I was a young high school student, I worked in a bakery at a time when that kind of work had to be done at night so our rolls and bread would be fresh for the daytime. We bakers were also on the Greenville, Ohio, informal volunteer fire department — that mainly meant we would follow the fire trucks on their runs. Several times after the yeast had been placed in the dough, we would leave in a hurry to watch or help on the fire truck stationed nearby. If it took very long to put out the fire, we would return to the bakery to find our little batch of dough had expanded many times and was all over the bench and the floor around it. At the time we added yeast to the dough it seemed such an insignificant little bit of something — but oh, how it grew!

Jesus promises that kind of result in his kingdom. "The kingdom of heaven is like yeast that a woman took and mixed into a large amount of flour until it worked all through the dough" (Matthew 13:33). Or he said, "The kingdom of heaven is like a mustard seed: when it grows, it is the largest of garden plants and becomes a tree ..." (Matthew 13:32).

It's an important understanding for us who want to be faithful disciples: The coming of God's kingdom causes a transformation in our individual lives as dramatic as yeast in dough, and in the lives of communities like little Neuendettelsau, Germany. And it most often starts with tiny, insignificant, what the world would call unimportant, beginnings.

So when the refugees are starving by the millions, we don't hesitate to give our little ten dollar contribution to World Hunger. When so many youth in our culture are abused, we can offer to be foster parents or big brothers or sisters for one. And when drug addiction and alcohol abuse is rampant in our community, we support and volunteer to help at the church's new teen center. And when the community asks for volunteers, or collections like United Way are taken, or when all the other well-intentioned efforts at making things better are attempted, we report for duty no matter how small our contribution. For in the working of the kingdom, God can do great things with what others would consider inconsequential, not big enough to make a difference.

Sometimes such little things as a thank you note or some flowers or a phone call of appreciation or support balloons into large acts of kindness which are then often practiced by others more skeptical as well.

Christianity can and does bring about big changes in lives. Consider the constant seeking of peace. Consider the mean marriages changed into loving partnerships. Think of the addictions overcome.

Then there are the transformations of hateful people into kind ones and greedy folks into ones who graciously share. And whole communities can be changed with Christian leaven, changed to love people of different skin color, culture, and ethnic heritage than our own. The homeless and battered and abused can be sheltered from the cold. The hungry can be fed.

27

And it's not because we began a little bit of the kingdom here with great big designs. It's just that we took what little we could do and trusted that these simple parables of Jesus were correct descriptions of how it is in the kingdom — little does grow into much and sometimes almost unseen and usually unheralded.

That's the way it was in little Neuendettelsau, Germany, when Johann Conrad Wilhelm Loehe arrived to begin his ministry. The tiny community was changed beyond even Loehe's wildest dreams. Individual lives were never the same again. That's always the way it's been in the kingdom: small, unpromising beginnings become dramatic, large results.

Look at how God worked it out to provide our forgiveness, salvation, a spiritual help here, and eternal life beyond the grave. It was an unpromising beginning in a limestone cave in Bethlehem, a ridiculed new kind of ministry, a resented-by-the-religious relationship with the church, and finally, a disgraceful crucifixion as a common criminal. But look how the world and our own lives have been changed because of those inauspicious beginnings.

The third parable is equally clear. This man who found a treasure and bought the field had his priorities right. He spent a lot to buy the field so now he obtained his treasure. This says to us that sacrifice is appropriate in certain cases of kingdom work. In a day of "get what's coming to you," and "don't let anyone take advantage of you," we have here a lesson in kingdom priorities which says that for some things it's still worth paying a big price.

We all should think about the causes and creature comforts for which we would sacrifice our lives — a bigger home, more and bigger cars, a second place to live, a boat, camper, golf clubs. This list could go on and on.

Because of this parable, we must search our souls about what price we and our family ought to pay in order to have what our culture says we should have to be happy. Often we are much older before we realize that real joy does not come from possessing things but in quality relationships with others.

Let's not forget that while Jesus told these as parables for his disciples, we are also disciples and we, too, must find ways to plant seed, even if it's very small. And we, too, must mix in and be the leaven for the whole loaves. God has called us to be workers in the kingdom too.

On the other hand, Jesus teaches here that there are treasures on earth for which we ought to sacrifice. It's not a popular idea right now. But it's a kingdom truth. For God's church, our individual ministries, and our priceless families, we ought to be willing to pay the price even when it means real sacrifice on our part.

Jesus told it in parable style: "The kingdom of heaven is like treasure hidden in a field. When a man found it ... in his joy he went and sold all he had and bought that field" (Matthew 13:44).

In many instances we who sacrifice are the ones who really benefit. To tithe, to give extra time to serve in our church, to help someone else, all benefits the other person. But in the kingdom as it starts small and grows and grows, we also benefit from doing the sacrificial giving of our money, our time, and our abilities for others. Sharing our whole self is very much called for in God's kingdom, which we pray might be here, just like in heaven.

There is a flip side to this parable that perhaps we don't often consider. In Neuendettelsau, where Loehe preached his whole ministry and such great kingdom work developed which still continues, there is a dark side as well.

During World War II, when Hitler's Nazis had control of Franconia, nearly 1,400 physically- and mentally-challenged children were bussed from the village's institutions to Germany's horrible gas chambers with the cooperation of the institution's director and some staff. That which had begun as kingdom work was turned into evil work.

In a nearby village where attempts were made to do the same thing, the director and staff courageously refused to cooperate. But in Loehe's little village, those special ones in the kingdom were sent to their premature deaths to the shame of all.

So here we discover the other side of these brief parables. Small beginnings like a mustard seed, the introduction of the minute into the whole like the yeast, and the paying of a sacrificial price for our treasure cannot be only for the coming of God's kingdom. It can also be, in similar fashion, for *the coming of evil into the world and our lives.*

Oh, how small and seemingly inconsequential a flirtation, then a promiscuous touch in the wrong place can be; but soon it might develop into adultery. How easily we can allow our language to be perverted into blasphemy against God. And in the congregation here, first a few negative comments about a brother or sister in Christ, then partaking in spreading rumors, and finally, full blown disruptive dissension which eats away at any maturing of the congregational kingdom work.

There is a power which naturally works against the power of God and God's kingdom. We can name the destructive power original sin, human nature, the demonic, or other such names. But it is always present, trying to grow — like this small mustard seed — into full bloom.

It wants, by its very nature, to influence the whole congregation of disciples like the leaven also! And sometimes, it seems to me, our tendency is to sacrifice a lot for its infection into our congregation. Sometimes it seems as though we will spend more of our energy in spreading gossip and bad news than in witnessing to the good news of the gospel. Sometimes it seems like our very human nature is to help the evil grow and delight in it more than the good and wholesome.

- Instead of loving our neighbor, we sow suspicion and hatred.
- Instead of praying for our enemies, we plot ways to get even.
- Instead of going the extra mile, we don't help at all.
- Instead of turning the other cheek, we strike back in revenge.
- Instead of loving the unlovely, we insist they must deserve our love.

It's a flip side not often spoken from pulpits these days and yet it is so real and we sacrifice our lives for it. It influences the whole congregation and community and though it starts small, it grows large.

It's been over fifty years now since those children were bussed to the gas chambers. In a town where a great preacher had a great vision of what God's kingdom could be, those buses remind us that all the good done in that village of mercy can also be perverted into an ugly demonic evil! Let it be our warning as well.

And might we have a vision here, like that of a Franconian preacher named Loehe, as we are warned and encouraged by these three wonderful kingdom parables of Jesus.

Grace
Isn't Fair

Matthew 20:1-16

So this fellow up in Sonoma County, not far from wine-growing Napa County, anxiously watched the weather forecast. Heavy rains of November were on the way across the Pacific. The grapes were mature and ready for harvest. Having no regular work crew, he went in to the union hall to get day laborers to do the picking. They agreed to work for ten dollars per hour. But the work didn't go fast enough and the sky was darkening with black clouds. Several times during the day he added more and more workers until the harvest was safely in the winery's barn.

Then the trouble began. Instead of paying the first to be hired, the foreman made them wait until last. Not only that, he paid those last to arrive the same amount as those who worked all day in that hot California sun. Those who worked all day and got only what they had agreed upon were angry. No doubt one of those California boycotts was certain to be organized against this Sonoma winery.

It's a parable of Jesus that only Matthew tells and it is a monument to unfairness! I sometimes wish Matthew had forgotten to write it down! On the other hand, it's one of the greatest of parables to teach us about ourselves and especially about how God is and wants to deal with us.

I believe Matthew, who wrote primarily a Gospel for teaching in the early church, had a very special purpose for including this one. He wanted to make sure that those who had entered the Christian Church early, like the disciples of Pentecost, didn't feel they were more important in God's sight than those who came into the faith much later on.

We can see how this could have been a problem. Those who knew Jesus face to face and had given up a lot to follow him must have been tempted to think they were just a little better than those who joined much later and didn't pay nearly the price in their lives to be Christian. To them the parable of the "Workers in the Vineyard" could be read again and again.

Evidently Matthew, who also wrote his Gospel as an appeal to the Jews, wanted them to know that while they were God's chosen and special people and had come into the vineyard early, others like the Gentiles were also acceptable to God and would have the same benefit as those who came first.

If this parable doesn't upset our normal way of thinking, we probably don't understand it. The parables always ought to challenge us to a new way of looking at our normal set of values and manner of living out our Christian faith. If we don't get a new perspective and challenge, we probably didn't comprehend the story. This particular parable of hiring workers for the vineyard is no exception. It tells us a lot about ourselves.

We have this natural way of thinking in us which says there should be merit and earning in what we receive. To this idea God says no — there should be grace. We want to give to those who *deserve* it. God wants us to share with others because they *need* it, not deserve it. It's a radical new way of looking at life itself. I help because they need the help.

Our tendency is to accept what our culture tells us, like: "They'll never appreciate it," or "You're wasting your time and money on those who don't deserve it," or "You'll never see them again."

If we do give to those who haven't earned or deserved it, we're often called "do-gooders and bleeding hearts." But that's exactly what Jesus asks us to do and to be in this parable of grumbling and late-coming vineyard workers.

The Christian who helps in a calculating way, figuring if it will be used wisely, or is deserved, or if there will be any resulting appreciation shown, will not ever be able to give with joy as the New Testament asks us to do. Still, we try to give that way and it's not a pleasant way to practice our discipleship. We'll always be like those resentful day laborers whom Jesus described, "... they began to grumble against the landowner" (Matthew 20:12a).

Now before we look at what this story tells us about God's graceful generosity, let's consider the flip side of the parable. It's all about our need to share in a very gracious manner. *It's not so much the need of those laborers to receive the abundant salary as the vineyard owner's need to give it to them!* How's that for a different way of looking at things?

The owner of that vineyard not only owned the real estate, but also had a big harvest coming in — all this wealth — when many men were standing all day in the village square desperately needing work to feed their hungry families! So he really needed to give away a lot in his life right then to keep a proper perspective and to keep his priorities from being all greed, selfishness, and possession accumulation.

Who was really blessed that day? Well, those who were fortunate to find a day's work with wages for it; those who worked only a part of a day and were overpaid. But the owner, who paid much more than fairness dictated, was the one I think was really blessed because of his compassion and generosity. And not because he planned and did it to be blessed, but because the generous giver who gives that way is always blessed without ever expecting it. He needed very much to share his wealth, and when he did, he was blessed because of it.

I imagine late that evening he was a better husband to his wife, a better father to his children, a better employer to his employees, with a quiet sense of joy in his successful harvest and a right understanding of stewardship the next week in his synagogue. The wine produced probably tasted all the sweeter!

I'm quite sure this has something crucial to say to us who live in such a consumer-driven culture and wealthy country. Our need is to *give*, much more than the church's or individual's or cause's need is to have our money or talents. We almost always get it backwards and talk about the church's need to have our offering. We ought to be praying about our need to give it away — and in large amounts so it makes a difference in our life's priorities. It's the primary way we stewards and disciples can keep our sanity in such an insane consumer-oriented society.

The danger is that we coldly calculate the *least* we need do to be respectful, and never know the benefits which that vineyard owner received because of his generosity to undeserving day laborers. That's probably not what Jesus had in mind when he first told this story which Matthew thought worth writing down. But it's what we need to hear on the flip side of the story.

The real heart and the main side of this parable is the wonderful grace of God. It tells us how God is and how God wants to deal with us. We are the undeserving late-comers who get much more than earned that day. God is no bookkeeper about what we deserve. God is a grace-filled generous benefactor who gives and gives and gives. And that same God also has compassion when we have needs like those day-laborers who stood in the village square waiting to be hired.

This story says to us that we never need to worry that we are alone in our struggles and desperation and that our needs are known by a loving God who has not kept track of our sins. Like the vineyard owner who saw those sad and desperate out-of-work laborers and invited them to come to his vineyard, so God sees us and bids us to come into the garden because of what the Christ did on the cross, ultimately coming out of the grave that first Easter Sunday. We just haven't earned that kind of gift, but God gives it *anyhow*.

Because of these basic teachings of the grace and compassion of God, this parable is one of the most significant of them all. Perhaps the one about the loving father (often called the prodigal son) would rank right up there as well, as it brings us a similar message of undeserved grace and forgiveness.

When we render the good service offered to us by the church, let's remember that we do it not because it earns us God's favor, but rather we do it out of thankfulness for a God who has already worked it out for us to have much more than we will ever deserve.

I hope those late-comers, who got much more pay than they deserved that day, later said and did some good things in that same vineyard the next time they traveled by it. I hope they were good stewards of the denarius given each. I hope if that landowner got in some kind of trouble they would want to help as a proper response to the grace given them that day.

Just one more thing about this story (which Jesus probably didn't have in mind at all). It too would be on the flip side of the parable. There is an example here of an attitude of boss to worker which is worth noting. Some of us are given the responsibility of supervising others. There is a special Christian stewardship in that which we ought to take seriously.

If we employ people, we are responsible for their very livelihood. We are not over them in order to be powerful tyrants, but stewards of their talents and abilities. We ought to see it as our ministry to care about them and their families in a compassionate way. What we pay them and how we treat them often shapes their family life and very human existence. To be the boss carries heavy responsibility. To own the vineyard was the same, and this owner did it well.

It's a great story and sounds like it could have happened in wine country in California. It certainly did happen there in Palestine. It tells us on its flip side to be compassionate managers of people and that our need to share is even bigger than others' need to have. On the main side, there is the wonderful example of the undeserved grace of God which is offered to us late-comers in the vineyard. There are also those admonitions not to calculate in our giving and to be careful how we think of those who join us even at the last hour.

Each time we receive the bread and wine undeserved, let us remember those workers who produced wine by picking grapes on a rocky, hot Palestine hillside and were blessed beyond what they deserved that day. Ours will be the same.

Some Tenants Are Better Than Other Tenants

Matthew 21:33-46

Some tenants are a lot better than other tenants. I found that out when, as a lad, I worked up the road on a farm owned by Walter and Esther Hupman. My job was to help candle eggs gathered on their egg route and exercise their English saddle horses.

The Hupmans couldn't begin to do all the farming themselves so they always had tenants living in a little house next to their unusual round barn. For farming the land the Hupmans owned, the tenants got to live in the house and receive a certain percentage of the income from the harvest.

Sometimes this arrangement worked better than other times. When a family moved out of the tenant house and on to another job, it was my task to clean up the house, barn, and property in preparation for new tenants. Some left everything clean, orderly, and ready for the next occupants.

When others left, I had an ugly job of cleaning out the trash, repainting the walls, repairing the flooring and outside gates, and so on. Evidently they took no responsibility for that which they did not own. Sometimes I wondered whether, had they owned it, they would have kept it any better. Some tenants are just a lot better than other tenants.

Jesus also told a story recorded by Matthew, Mark, and Luke about lousy tenants. These worked a vineyard whose owner lived outside of the country. But when he sent servants to collect his portion of the earnings, the tenants "... beat one, killed another and stoned a third" (Matthew 21:35).

A second group of servants were also treated the same way. So the owner sent his son, thinking surely they would respect him. But Matthew says, "So they took him and threw him out of the vineyard and killed him" (Matthew 21:39).

Some tenants are a lot better than other tenants!

This parable told by Jesus is one of the very few which we ought to dissect and assign meanings to many of its parts. Usually we just concentrate on one main theme, but here we look at several parts:

— Vineyard is the nation of Israel.
— Owner of vineyard represents God.
— Tenants represent religious leaders of the day.
— Messengers represent the Old Testament prophets.
— Son represents Jesus the Christ.

So when Jesus first told this story he certainly wanted to prepare his disciples for what was coming. The leaders of Judaism were God's chosen people and workers in God's vineyard. "The vineyard of the Lord Almighty is the house of Israel, and the men of Judah are the garden of his delight" (Isaiah 5:7).

But they did not listen to the message of the prophets. They would even kill God's son who came to establish God's kingdom. Jesus claimed the vineyard would be given over to the Christian church. At least that's the way it has been interpreted after Easter by us Christians.

The story tells us much about us humans. God gives us a lot of freedom. Notice these tenants could work this vineyard as they pleased. They had the freedom to be their own people and do it the way they best devised.

But also notice there did come a time when they were held accountable for their keeping of the owner's vineyard. This says to me that while we have the freedom to live our Christian lives as we wish, there is also a time when we must give an account of how well we have lived on God's behalf.

It also tells me that you and I are really privileged. We, in our country and culture, are given a rich vineyard in which to live and work. Jesus says this vineyard in which these tenants worked had a wine press, a wall around it, a watchtower in which to live, and all that was really needed to do their task and live well.

We also learn about us humans that we often want to take our own way even when we know God's way is quite different. Our bullheadedness to do what we want deliberately — when God wants something quite different — compares to those tenants who continued to fail to give the owner his share of the profits. But then some tenants are better than other tenants, aren't they?

The story also tells us some nice things to know about God. God is trusting. We are given the vineyard and are trusted to care for it without the owner looking over our shoulder. And God is very patient, sending messengers over and over even though they are badly treated. Finally, he sends his son, thinking, "They will respect my son" (Matthew 21:37b).

How good it is to know we have that kind of trusting and patient God when we lose confidence in ourselves and when we feel guilt for our behavior. God trusts us and God is patient with us. Like a wonderful, loving parent, God gives us lots of latitude to practice our discipleship, especially since the cross of Calvary is patient.

Let's now turn to the other side of this parable, for it has such a relevant message for us now. Jesus told the story and Matthew wrote it down to illustrate how the religious leaders had rejected God's prophets sent to them to warn them about their behavior as citizens of the kingdom, also preparing them for the fact he would be killed by the religious of the day.

There is another message we can consider. *It's about the stewardship of the vineyard.* We have been given a wonderful earth on which to live and the creator continues to send to us messengers who say we ought to conserve and nurture this vineyard for its owner's (God's) sake and for the sake of future dwellers here to come long after us. It's a stewardship of creation which is called for. And we who are tenants in this Eden given to us by God ought to take seriously our sacred responsibility to deal gently with the earth and all its natural resources.

Even though God has given us great freedom to do as we please, we really have a tenant's responsibility not to use up, misuse, or overuse that which makes our lives so pleasant here. For the sake of the grandchildren and great grandchildren who come after us, let us care well for our fruitful vineyard. Sometimes I like to call it resource inheritance, meaning that which future generations will inherit because of our ecological and theological mindedness — or lack of it.

It's just not true that it's our property and we can do with it as we please. We are tenants on this planet for a short while, and those who come after us must rely on our conservation for the resources they inherit for their lives. It's much like those tenant farmers on the Hupman farm. Some left the house, barn, and facilities much better than when they moved in. Others did not. Some tenants are a lot better than other tenants.

In a day when we have become painfully aware of child abuse and sexual abuse in the human world, we now must become aware of abuse of the non-human world, like water, oil, natural gas, and other resources. Just as Jesus said that the Good Samaritan's neighbor was the man beaten and in the ditch, so soil erosion and rape of the rain forest are also our neighbors and in need of our intervention on their behalf. They have been beaten up, misused, and almost eliminated.

God's servants have come with warning after warning for us to change our lifestyle and attitudes to a better stewardship of the vineyard given us. God is trusting us to do it.

Because I live near the former California home of the greatest conservationist of the nation, John Muir, I have taken an interest in reading his hand-written journals in Martinez, California.

Over 100 years ago this devout outdoorsman, who is called the father of our national parks, wrote that while it was good to argue for preserving and conserving the national resources so future generations would have enough, there is a "deeper ecology." We care for the creation simply because it is God's. What a great concept! It takes us far beyond preservation — that our future relatives might have enough — to a spiritual perspective of preserving what is *not* ours to waste, but what is God's.

If we take this story Jesus told of wicked tenants in a vineyard and turn it upside down, we soon see it speaks to us who often selfishly squander the limited resources of our vineyard. And the results one day might be as drastic as those tenants throwing out the owner's servants and killing the son!

We really can't say we haven't been warned. Ecological servants have been coming to us for a number of years now, sounding the clear alarm that we are soiling our own nest and fouling that which has in the past been lovely.

Yet we read in the Old Testament that God created it all and for a short time is putting us in charge. We have taken too far the biblical command to "Be fruitful and increase in number; fill the earth and subdue it" (Genesis 1:28), and we have not taken our responsibilities seriously enough where we are told to "Rule over the fish of the sea and the birds of the air and over every living creature that moves on the ground" (Genesis 1:29).

It's just not a pious option any longer if we are God's tenant. We must practice good family planning and population control, even with all the problems that presents. Right now the growth rate is two percent. That means the population will double in the next 35 years. In 56 years, it will triple, and in 117 years it will have increased ten times!

Andy Rooney, on *60 Minutes*, said, "There are more people on the earth right now than ever lived and died here." If God would rewrite the Old Testament now, instead of "Be fruitful and multiply," God would say, "Enough already!" Our world cannot support this kind of growth. It is too fragile and limited in its resources.

As Americans we can no longer continue using up so much of the world's resources to support our lavish lifestyles. There are simpler ways of living which will consider the other inhabitants of this globe.

All the flip side of this parable has a lot to say to me about how I live out my tenancy on this earth beginning with such things as how high I eat on the food chain, how many cars and creature comforts I gather around me, whether I really make a concerted effort to recycle, the sprays I use, the electricity I consume. This list could go on and on.

I believe that the younger generation is probably better informed and motivated to live this way than we older ones who just never dreamed it was necessary. And we are often the ones who beat up the messengers sent to us by calling them hippies and flower children of no consequence.

Those of my lifetime have seen such wonderful scientific breakthroughs that we supposed all along God would work through scientists to solve our problems of resource depletion and pollution. But now we are learning that the scientific solutions often have a flip side which is negative and exacerbates, rather than solves, the problem.

A few years ago the green revolution quadrupled our production of food, especially in middle America. Now the creeks run foul with poisoned fish and the water has a head, foaming from all the chemicals which leach into it.

One of the marvelous things about the parables of Jesus is that in any age they have a way of raising the basic questions with which we ought to be struggling as Christians. This one about ungrateful tenants really packs a wallop for today.

On the flip side, it admonishes us to be good caretakers of creation. On the main side, it tells us God is patient and trusting, and that God gives us great freedom which brings great responsibility. Jesus first told it to warn the disciples that he and the kingdom would be rejected to the serious danger of those who did the rejecting.

Some tenants are a lot better than other tenants. I learned that at Hupman's farm when I had to clean up and repair after tenants moved out. I learned it again as I studied this parable of Jesus about a vineyard and how those appointed took care of it.

Joy, Grace,
And Living Together

Matthew 22:1-14

Chirpy was a parakeet. Cleaning the cage one day, the owner was disturbed by the telephone, got the hose of the vacuum cleaner too close and sucked the bird right into the sweeper bag. Quickly she hung up, took off the bag, pulled out the bewildered bird, and stuck it under the water faucet. The bird survived, but now its owner describes it this way: "Chirpy doesn't sing much anymore, she just sits and stares."

Our church has many who don't sing much anymore, if they ever did, but just sit and stare. Today's parable of a wedding reception is for them and us.

Matthew and Luke thought it important enough to record it sometime after Jesus told the story. It was probably first aimed at the religious of Jesus' day who refused his invitation to God's kingdom. He had come to invite them into it and they refused the invitation.

So he told this story to say that like a man who invited many to his son's wedding celebration and no one came, so too, he came with an invitation to the religious to come into God's kingdom and no one came. So, he said, others must be invited.

In the parable as he told it, the father of the groom sent out servants with this inclusive instruction: " 'Go to the street corners and invite to the banquet anyone you find.' So the servants went out into the streets and gathered all the people they could find, both good and bad, and the wedding hall was filled with guests" (Matthew 22:8, 10).

This ought to be an encouraging parable for us. For it says much about how and who we should invite into God's kingdom. It tells us the invitation is one to joy. That's where Chirpy the parakeet comes in. If you feel you've been through the vacuum cleaner and your baptismal water washed you but did not bring joy; if the practice of your discipleship is rather bland, uninteresting, and of little relevance to real life — this parable is for you.

If we get nothing else said today, let's say this loud and clear: we are invited into a life of joy. The great preacher George A. Buttrick used to say, "Joy is what we are chosen for and joy is what we have to offer to all who will come. It is a deep sense of joy not dependent on the number of things we get done in a day, for this is not the opposite of unhappiness but the opposite of unbelief."

The invitation was not to a funeral wake, but a wedding feast! Sometimes in our sense of awe and reverence we give out the wrong signal about Christianity — it looks grim, depressing, and downright dismal, like Chirpy after her vacuum cleaner experience.

I preached in Curran Memorial Church in Sanoyea, Liberia, one dark night. There were no lights in the church, except for the ones the several hundred villagers brought with them. They placed a Coleman gasoline lantern in front of me so the congregation could see me as I spoke. The lantern kept running down and a deacon kept pumping it up during my sermon with the comment, "Preach on."

After the service — and I had preached for an hour — the elder of the congregation led us through the town with lanterns, the Kpella choir dancing and playing sassas, drums, and animal horns tapped with a stick. Here was joy-filled, celebrated Christianity — and to those who watched us that night there was no doubt about our joy in the Lord as we sang in the Kpella language: "Where are we going? We are going to God's Village."

Chirpy the parakeet had lost such joy which made her sing, and perhaps we too who gather here. But as Jesus told in his parable of a father and his wedding feast for his son — it's joy to which we are invited and joy into which we have the privilege of inviting others.

Perhaps it's the preachers' fault that we often miss the joy of discipleship. We often deal with such sad, grim issues like death and illness that we soon take on the aura of undertakers and criminal judges. However, the invitation is to a celebration, a feast, a joy-filled wedding.

Sometimes we give off the perception that this Christian joy is what we obtain when we die rather than having it right now. Like so many of the New Testament promises, we read them as something that, if we are good enough, we'll have in the future.

Consider Matthew's listing of Jesus' preaching themes called the Beatitudes in chapter 5. When we read them in a "stained glass" voice it sounds as if it will happen in the "sweet by-and-by" rather than right now while at the wedding feast to which we have been invited.

The Beatitudes could very well be translated: Oh, the joy of the poor in spirit, those who mourn, the meek, those who hunger and thirst for righteousness, the merciful, and the pure in heart. Oh, the joy of the peacemakers and those who are persecuted. It's joy now for them and for us.

These are not promises for the future but congratulations on how it can be for Christians in God's kingdom here in the present. It's even joy for such as Chirpy the parakeet who got sucked into a vacuum cleaner, doused with water, and just doesn't sing much anymore. Perk up, sad bird, and sing again with us for we have joy.

There is something else in this parable that preachers over the years have called attention to. Those who did not come to the wedding reception probably had fairly good reasons not to do so. One went to his field no doubt to cultivate or water the crop and another went to his business. Everyone knows when you are in business you must be there to make it a successful one. It's a warning we busy Americans all need to hear. Second best can often crowd out the very best.

We must watch out as we set our priorities. That which is okay can often crowd out that which is critically important, like parenting, worship, marriage relationships, and stewardship. It's not the central message here but one you and I very much need to take seriously. The old adage that we should be careful lest "making a living crowd out making a life" is still worth taking to heart.

If in this parable we let the wedding banquet represent the holy communion feast in our church, then we have real reason to consider what crowds out our being here at this feast of Christ's presence when we remember what God did for us in Jesus on Calvary's cross, Easter's empty tomb, and Pentecost's Spirit blessing. The list could be long on why we turn down this gracious invitation to eat bread and drink wine together, and experience the Christ with us like no other time in our lives.

It is an invitation of grace, isn't it? We don't deserve to be here and we don't deserve to have God do for us what has already been done in our salvation and empowerment to live life to the fullest now. But still God invites us anyhow, just as that king had his servants invite those on the street corners in his day. They weren't relatives; they hadn't contributed to his campaign for king; and they didn't know the bride or groom. Still, they were asked to the feast. We are, too. And perhaps even sad, ruffled-feathers Chirpy also!

Now, what could be the flip side of this story of joy and graciousness? Each of these parables, if we dig deep enough, has a secondary message that may be beneficial to us in our day as well. I believe this parable's flip side is how those undeserving guests, who were invited into such joy as a wedding reception, had a special challenge. *How were they to live together after the party?*

Years ago in a church magazine question-and-answer column, there was debate about whether in Lutheran churches the ushers should guide the people out after worship. I'll never forget one letter to the editor which profoundly commented like this: "Usher them in? Usher them out? I say lock the doors and see if they can live with each other!"

That's the question here. How do we relate to each other, we who have been given such an undeserved gift of grace and celebration of joy? Our answer has to be that the same kind of undeserved grace given us we should give each other. The same kind of joy given us we should offer to each other. Jesus' admonitions to love one another, to turn the other cheek, to go the extra mile, to pray for each other, to be kind, and so on, are directions for how we treat each other who also have not deserved the forgiveness, the eternal life, and the spirit with us now so graciously given.

To have this undeserved grace means not only a certain profound joy, but also a big responsibility. It dictates gracious behavior to others, especially when they don't deserve it.

It also tells us who and how we invite to join us in God's present kingdom. They don't need to look or act like us. They don't need to be society's well-accepted or the community's majority (if it has one). They don't have to be of our culture or what we call "our people." They don't have to be those who "fit in" or behave as we should.

We just invite because we have been invited. And then we do our best to see that others experience the joy which has so enriched our own lives. It's the joy which is the opposite of unbelief. It's the joy Chirpy lost in the vacuum cleaner and under the water faucet. It's the joy I experienced deep in the Sumatran jungle.

We arrived at Tapiannauli, the Bona ni Pinasa (village of origin) of one of my Batak Christian seminary students. After catechizing approximately 150 on Saturday evening, we drank coffee they had grown and roasted, then we sang. A beautiful kebaya-clad girl named Omega stood and sang out hymn after hymn to familiar tunes. The next morning I preached a naked, simple gospel: of Jesus born in Bethlehem, a godly ministry in Galilee, sacrifice on the cross for our forgiveness, Easter resurrection — that we too might come out of the grave — and then returned in Spirit to be with us here now.

And then while the old women chewed napuran, we sang and celebrated the presence of that same Spirit with us still. A pig was killed and a hula hula (celebration) held. We ate sac-sang and they presented me with an ulas (cloth of deep friendship).

That simple, without-frills Christianity touched me deeply as we sang hymns of joy in God's presence. It was "the basics" at Tapiannauli bush village and it was full of joy.*

So we return to where we started in this sermon about Jesus' story of a wedding feast where everyone was invited. Living together afterward must have been the hardest part. But we must, and we have help.

To have this kind of invitation to joy is also a big responsibility. And when life sucks us into the vacuum cleaner like Chirpy — we can still sing again.

———————————

*Illustrations used in this sermon are from Schmalenberger's book of stories and metaphors titled *These Will Preach,* CSS Publishing, 1999, pp. 74-75.

In Celebration Of
The One-Talent Person

Matthew 25:14-30

Some parables of Jesus are really upsetting. This is one of those. But then, that's what parables are supposed to do: challenge our normal way of thinking. If understood, they question our present priorities and punch us in the stomach like a hammer with a different way of considering a situation.

Here is a story told by Jesus and written down for us by Matthew and Luke which performs all these radical actions.

A man was leaving the country for a while so he gave five bags of money to one person, two bags to another, and one bag to a third. When he returned and asked for an accounting of their stewardship, those people who were given five or two bags had invested wisely (or were very lucky) and doubled the absentee landlord's wealth.

Then comes the central focus of the story which makes me very uncomfortable, as a parable should. The poor fellow who had received only one bag was afraid to risk investing it and thus hadn't gained a penny. He returned just what he had received.

The owner was angry and according to Matthew, said to the one-bag man: "You wicked, lazy servant! ... you should have put my money on deposit with the bankers so that when I returned I would have received it back with interest" (Matthew 25:26-27).

I'll have more to say later about why I don't like how this one-talent man was treated.

Why do you think Matthew and Luke wanted us to know this story? At the time I'll bet it was aimed at the scribes and Pharisees who were the super religious of the day. They thought of themselves as protectors of the faith and saw any change as threatening their position and their God. So Jesus said they were like this one-talented man who was not willing to risk. He saw his religion as something which demanded it remain exactly the same.

It's what eventually brought about Jesus' crucifixion outside Jerusalem's walls. The pillars of the church just couldn't stand being challenged — not in Jesus' claiming to forgive sins, not in his calling the dead out of their graves, and not in questioning the money exchange policies in the temple courtyard could they tolerate the newness. So in this story Jesus doesn't focus on the many-talented men and women who appear on the cover of *Time* and *Newsweek*, but he zeros in on this one-talented person cowering behind his skirts of littleness.

There are times when all of us are tempted to act like the one-talent person. We consider the little we have to offer, the minimal difference we could make, the risk in venturing out or trying something new and different, and we never get started at all. Yet, God depends on us with few talents. God wants us whether we have one, two, or five talents to take what we can contribute and offer it, trusting God will use it to great advantage.

Think of those great Bible heroes we hold up as models of the godly life and how imperfect and sometimes one-talented they were. And yet think what God was able to do through them because they trusted God would use whatever they offered, no matter how small or seemingly insignificant, to great advantage. If you took their halos off, they'd be a motley crew: Moses with a stammer in his tongue and blood on his hands; James and John, loud-mouthed fishermen boasting about their place in the kingdom; Peter, a big hulk of a man usually with his foot in his mouth; Paul, a beady-eyed, humpbacked, ugly man chasing the early Christians; and Luther, grumpy and very troubled by constipation in his old age. Oh, how God used the likes of these. God would like to work through us also.

Our temptation is to think we ought to bury our talent in the ground and keep it safe. We try our best to keep everything in our congregation as it was in the good old days when we were growing up. So we fight new forms of worship and music. We oppose trying new paradigms of ministry. We block attempts to reach the young generation with different approaches. We vote against the congregation's attempts to be dynamic and creative.

Jesus was aiming right at the religious of his day who fought change every inch of the way. He aims still at us when we try to do the same. He holds before us this pitiful little untalented man and says, "Be careful lest this be you."

Because the church is our place of precious memories, it's very tempting to behave like this one-talent man. We often feel we owe it to the past. We owe it to those who have gone before us — to our parents and grandparents, to the memories of our childhood, to keep it like that forever.

But the church must be a dynamic organization always applying the gospel to the present situation. We must continually update and risk experimentation in order to make our vital religion relevant in our time. When we keep it the same, like burying the one bag of money, it surely will cause the church to move from being a mission station to being a museum where we view the old, gold coins as a curiosity of days long gone.

Perhaps this is a valuable story for us today. It certainly points out the truth that we individuals are variously blessed with different amounts of talents. Some are so gifted and some have so much wealth. Some of us have much less. We must take it into account as we organize for ministries in our congregation. It's just not fair to ask a one-talented disciple to lead the choir when there are those who can do it so well.

And when it comes to wealth, there are some of us who could give a lot more. We can easily afford it and really need to share a lot more of what we have as a way of knowing the blessing of correct priorities. It's a way for us to live together. We recognize that each person is different and there are different ways each can and ought to help out as we serve in our ministries on God's behalf in the world.

There is a certain teaching here which is a little more difficult to understand. This story tells us that we ought to use our talents or we may be in danger of losing them. It's true in playing a musical instrument, playing a sport, speaking a foreign language, and many other talents. It's "use it or lose it." And those who have been blessed abundantly in sharing will find they are blessed with even more. Listen: "Take the talent from him and give it to the one who has the ten talents. For everyone who has will be given more, and he (she) will have an abundance" (Matthew 25:28-29).

Many years ago, before the Great Depression, a very wealthy man donated the money for a fine organ for his church in Toledo, Ohio. He lost everything he had during the depression of 1929 and was forced to take a job as janitor in his church during the sad 1930s. I've been told you could go in that church and hear him playing the organ he had given. He became well known for saying that what he had kept he lost, but what he had given away he still had. It's a point of this parable as well.

The story seems to say to me that the reward for doing a good work is more work to do. We preachers know that to be the case in our ministries. But this seems to say it is also true for all the people of God as we work together. While we must be careful lest we burn out and work to death the five- and ten-talented folks, we also must recognize that's the way it is in the kingdom — good job well done means another and even larger job to do!

I've tried to come up with a pithy way of summarizing the heart of this story with the traditional interpretation. It's simply that the one who is punished is the one who wouldn't try.

There is a flip side to this story I'm anxious to explore with you. I doubt either of these items is often proclaimed the way this parable is assigned to us: *We all have a ministry using our talents given to us and we need to be a lot more sensitive toward the one-talented person than this owner was.*

When we speak of ministry we immediately think of what the preacher should or shouldn't do. But isn't it true here that God calls each one of us to identify what our gifts, abilities, and wealth are and use them in a ministry we practice every day of the week?

So it's not only here under the church roof as we do all those things we must do to carry out our life of faith together, but it's also what we do the rest of the days of the week where and when we work, live, and play. Some have been given the natural ability to make peace, some to pray, some to love the unlovely, some to teach, some to witness to their faith, some to feed and clothe the

54

poor. The list is endless. Through our baptism we have been called to be ministers in the world and apply our talents given us (one or ten) in order that God's kingdom might be lived out through them and us.

When we gather for worship, it's not so much if we like it or not, but rather how we can help each other identify our talents and give encouragement to go out another six days and minister with what we have been given, trusting God will use it in marvelous ways beyond our wildest expectations.

Now the flip side which won't be found in any Bible commentary or heard from any other pulpit: This owner who gave out the talents "... each according to his ability" (Matthew 25:15b) should have been a lot more sensitive to the feelings and abilities of that one-talent person! Perhaps this poor soul just wasn't smart enough to invest with the bankers. Perhaps all his life he had been told he was inadequate and thus did not have the self-confidence to do more than hide and thus protect the one bag of money.

I believe *this story illustrates a certain lack of compassion and understanding which should have been there all along.* The one-talent person did not waste or lose the money. Have some compassion for the little guy here! Jesus taught that in many ways. How could Matthew let this come through to us in this way? I celebrate the one-talent servant today.

In congregations like ours we must always be sensitive to those who feel inadequate, under-educated, or of less wealth than the rest. They, too, are God's called disciples. It's much more difficult for some than others to live the life of a disciple. It's harder for some to risk, to venture out, to be faithful in Bible study, worship, and prayer than others. It's easier for some to go the extra mile or turn the other cheek or pray for and love their enemies than it is for others. We must accept them too, and not judge them harshly because it's easy for us.

If I had been Matthew I would have wanted to rewrite this story to end something like this: "His master replied to the person given one talent, 'I'm sorry you saw me as such a hard man gathering where I have not sown. I'll try to show you a different side of my behavior more consistent with how I believe God wants us to be. Take this one talent you have saved of mine and meet with the servant to whom I gave five and ask him to help you learn how to invest it. There are better ways to use your talent than to bury it in the ground. For everyone who has much will be encouraged to share with those who have little or none at all. Bring the servant in from the darkness where there is weeping and gnashing of teeth that he might also share in our joy.' "

It's dangerous to try to rewrite scripture, but you might think about this flip side which says we all have a ministry to share and we need to be sensitive to the many one-talented people as well as to the multi-talented people. So we add this to the main focus of talent use which includes these thoughts: we often lose what we don't use; we must be careful about our resistance to change; and we are blessed differently with a variety of gifts to be used for the kingdom.

Safer Roads
And Real Life

Luke 10:25-37

Maybe the priest and the Levite were the smartest after all. They were well-disciplined, educated people who had learned to be cautious on the road to Jericho. It was a treacherous stretch of road winding down from Jerusalem around sand hills, boulders with good places for robbers to hide, attack, and escape. When they saw their fellow Jew there in the ditch beaten and nearly dead, it was the prudent thing to do to be careful. After all:
— This might be a decoy for the robbers.
— Someone might think they were the robbers.
— They may have to use all their money paying the innkeeper.
— Besides now they will be late for church.
Then a Samaritan came along:
— The Samaritan might be rejected by this Jew.
— Later other Samaritans might disapprove of his aid.
It's probably one of the most familiar stories in all the Bible. It is without parallel in all the Gospels. Jesus told it as the answer to an expert in law who asked, "And who is my neighbor?" (Luke 10:29b).

And so this parable of the Good Samaritan has even found its way into our governmental law with so-called "Good Samaritan" laws to protect someone who stops to help another in trouble. I know owners of travel trailers have "Good Samaritan Clubs" whose members promise to help each other, also.

We know, along with this expert in the law, that we are to love our neighbor as Jesus' disciples. What we're not as sure about: Who is our neighbor here in our day and in this place? It seems to me there is a whole list of neighbors who are in need and thus must have our help.

— The prisoners in our jails.
— The victims of child abuse.
— Those infected with AIDS.
— The mentally challenged on our streets.
— The refugees around this war-torn world.
— The hungry in whatever ditch they lie.
— Those with different sexual preferences than ours.

The radical part of this story is not only in the definition of the neighbor we love as anyone who is beaten and in the side ditch of life, but that we should care for them even when they don't like us and we don't like them!

Our tendency is to help that person who will appreciate it and thank us for it. We most want our neighbor to be like us and be lovable. But in this very radical story, Jesus claims for us a different way of looking at our discipleship. I'll bet he was looking at his own followers as he told the story, hoping they would catch on to this new, radical, revolutionary way of serving God and God's people.

The Samaritan was good not only for helping someone, but especially for assisting a Jew. The Jews hated what they considered "half-breed Samaritans" and the feeling was mutual from the Samaritan side as well. Picture those two down in the Jericho roadside ditch! It was a lot for the expert in the law to digest.

On Martin Luther King, Jr. Day, Peter Jennings on the *ABC News* told how some years before when those little black girls were killed by the bombing at the Sixteenth Street Baptist Church in Birmingham, Alabama, the face of Jesus on its statue was also blown off. When we pass by our neighbor because of some hatred, we pass by the Christ as well. His image is destroyed.

Being a disciple of Christ really means being willing to risk. It means not playing it safe like the Levite and Priest did, no doubt with the approval of most of their congregational members.

Today the parable remains the same but the neighbors change somewhat. In a day of globalization when we can easily communicate and travel all over this world, in a day when the countries of the world become more and more multicultural, it's the same parable but with much longer side ditches.

As other world religions make their way into our culture, it's tempting to let prejudice against them creep into our very human nature. Christian, Muslim, Buddhist, Jew, Hindu, and agnostic all have occasions when life throws them into the ditch, and as disciples we become their neighbor.

Our nature has a way of wanting to separate and qualify who gets our compassion. Jesus said, "No," to this tendency. He said just keep your eye on the ditch at the side of the road and there you'll find plenty of neighbors to help. They may not speak our language or practice our customs or religion, or be from the same ethnic background. But they are our neighbors.

In some ways it's an impossible task asked of us. First we are told: "Love your neighbor as yourself" (Luke 10:27b) and then we are admonished that any person beaten up and suffering in the ditch is our neighbor. It's not difficult to love any neighbor who is lovely or who will love us in return. Now this story tells us to do it for those we even downright dislike and who don't deserve it at all!

Over the years preachers and Bible study leaders have railed against the Priest and Levite for passing by. It's true the practice of our religion can be so legalized that it lacks basic human compassion.

And it's also true we can get so engrossed with the busyness of being a Christian and a church member, and so weary of helping others, that our religion becomes uncaring and without compassion. This story stands for all eternity for Christians and non-Christians alike as an encouragement to continue to help and care. We must be careful lest we acquire the tough-hide syndrome. We can come to a place in our lives where we no longer are sensitive to the needs of others and especially those we just don't trust or like. Some have named it *compassion fatigue*.

And there are always rationalizations we can make to ourselves and others about why we don't help them like: "They brought it on themselves." The world will accept these excuses and, like the Priest and Levite, we'll remain in their eyes respectable. But the side ditch beckons still for our discipleship and ministry of compassion.

We have to ask the question today I think James and John, Peter and Andrew, and Mary Magdalene must have been asking: "Who am I in this parable?" Am I the busy religious leader who just doesn't have time to help? Am I the one beaten in the ditch who so desperately needs a neighbor and has come here today to find one? Am I the preacher who is late and has become insensitive to life's side ditches? Or am I the Samaritan whose heart rather than prejudices dictated his loving action? Even if he were a heretic, the charity of God was in his heart. He is now judged not by his creed but by the life he lived and the practical help he gave. Maybe I'm the robber who had no regard for human dignity and let greed rule my behavior? We all can find our place in this story today.

The Good Samaritan I have most admired during my lifetime has been Mother Teresa of Calcutta. It seems she could love on God's behalf without any need for the recipient to love her back or deserve the love. She knew that feeling sorry wasn't good enough — one must get down in the ditch and offer practical help.

I once witnessed such undeserved love given in Liberia, West Africa. The pastor was on sabbatical from his congregation and serving in Totota village while living in a small unequipped former missionary's house. There was a mentally deranged person named John whose legs were paralyzed so that he crawled on the ground dragging them behind him. At night John would scream outside the pastor's house all through the night, keeping him awake for hours.

When it came time for the clergyman to depart, as he left the house to get in a jeep that would take him to Monrovia and back to the U.S., John dragged himself up and began to scream obscenities at him and his wife. The pastor, observing the clothing on the cursing man, simply stopped, and opening his packed suitcase, emptied it of its contents, and gave them to John. There was a momentary earth-shattering silence as all there watched this twentieth century Samaritan.

There was no sign of appreciation or thanks from John. He cursed the pastor as he left. But the one who had shown the undeserved compassion is still known in that little Liberian village as Jesus' own disciple who helped one who disliked him.

Now let's turn to the other side of this story. It seems as though all the parables and miracles of Jesus usually have another side which is very instructive for us to consider, but which probably wasn't meant to be the main focus at the time they were told.

I believe the non-human world can also be in the ditch and badly abused and thus in need of our loving care. I have already mentioned that in an earlier sermon on the absentee landlord and the tenants titled "Some Tenants Are Better Than Other Tenants." Let it suffice here simply to say we humans have badly misused and wasted our natural resources and the animal kingdom. They are beaten and we need to love them back to health like the Good Samaritan did for the badly beaten Jew. And when it's time to pay the cost of their recovery, we need to do it cheerfully, like the Samaritan did to the innkeeper in this story.

The two items I see on the flip side of this parable are about *making the road safe and about real life.*

Notice in verses 27 and 28, we have these words: "Love your neighbor as yourself," and "Do this and you will live." Here is some vital advice about how to really live. Being cautious like the Priest and meticulous in religious ceremony like the Levite isn't living. It's existing in a dull, often judgmental and resentful mood. Here is a new way, Jesus said. He often gave us new ways to look at life and thus a possibility of a different existence.

The other side of this story says to me: try giving your life away for others; try giving practical help even to those who don't deserve it; try overcoming your petty prejudice and loving "anyhow" and see if that doesn't produce a new, abundant, fulfilling, peace-producing life for you and those you help. I just can't help hearing those words over and over to that expert in the law: "... do this and you will live" (Luke 10:27b).

Wow! Who here doesn't aspire to a fuller and richer life — real life? And here on the back side of a story about a "half-breed" helping his enemy, a Jew half dead from robbers, we find the key to real life for the followers of Jesus. Mother Teresa put it this way, "If life is not lived for others, it is not worthwhile."

There is one other element on the other side of this parable I want to hold before you. Each time I read or hear the story preached, it comes to my mind. Suppose the next time the Samaritan came down that road there was another victim of those robbers. And suppose after that, every time he traveled that way he found more and more beaten-up Jews in the ditch. It would be one thing to help them over and over, but it would be even more important to clean up the crime and *make the road safe for everyone.*

Frequently we need to do more than treat the symptoms of violence and patch up the wounded. We need to examine the systems and get at the heart of the evil. If Jews were being beaten on that road, a disciple would need to help set up community watch programs, help establish better policing, erect street lighting, etc.

Loving our neighbor often goes beyond the temporary first aid bandage. We can help start this action of loving our neighbor as well. It's not good enough to feed the hungry. We must find the cause of their hunger and help our society help them learn to support themselves.

If crime is a serious problem, we must look beyond holding Bible study for those in prison to seeing what is leading our folks to be arrested for misconduct, and find ways to bring them out of such circumstances.

If welfare checks are given out with no counsel on how to escape from this system that often demeans people and makes them dependent, we need to lead in the community to help make a difference.

If teen pregnancy is a problem, we need to do much more than care for the resulting unwanted children. We must help in the school and find ways in our church youth programming to avoid such haphazard conception and birth.

See this obvious flip side to the idea we should love the unlovely? It's a message powerfully needed in our day and in this congregation. The road needs to be made safe as much as the hated need to be loved and cared for. The non-human need love as well as the ungrateful and undeserving. And in all these is to be found a new religious and daily life for those of us who are "half dead," as the parable puts it.

Maybe the Priest and Levite and Christians were right to be so cautious. Maybe not! The expert in the law said it was "the one who had mercy on him" who was a real neighbor. Jesus says to us: "...: go and do likewise" (Luke 10:37).

The Never Lost
Ninety-Nine

Luke 15:1-10

The homemade sign hanging on a large construction crane outside Methodist Hospital in Des Moines, Iowa, said simply, "Linda is O.K." I was making my rounds in the hospital when I spotted it outside the window. I never found out who Linda was or from what threat she was now O.K., but I am confident a crane operator was rejoicing that day about some marvelous rescue of Linda.

Our parable today is a similar story. Because Jesus had been severely criticized for welcoming sinners and even eating with them, he told this story of a shepherd willing to go back out and search for one sheep out of 100 who was lost. It's not with any particular risk to the 99 safe in the fold. Other shepherds would watch after them, as often was the case in the communal sheep folds of Palestine.

This is basically a parable about getting lost and celebrating both the recovery and being found. Three of these "lost" stories follow in a row in Luke's fifteenth chapter. First this lost sheep, then a lost coin, then a lost son. There is a lot of celebration in the finding of the lost in all three stories. That was the point Jesus was making to those muttering about his taking up with the sinners.

God really celebrates the finding of those some consider lost. There is great joy over even one returning or coming for the first time to the safety of the fold. Jesus was saying to the super religious of his day to give up their criticism of those being rescued and rejoice with him their new life. It's like that in heaven, he said.

There is a lot of celebrating when even *one* who was lost is found. Notice this has a lot to tell us about Christian joy. The temptation is to try to figure out if the person is worth the effort. But here Jesus said this shepherd turned over 99 to other shepherds and went back out to search for one — and when he found the lost one, there was a lot of celebrating, like the crane operator outside the window at Methodist Hospital. Not only did the shepherd rejoice and the home village celebrate, but even God and heaven's angels rejoiced as well!

This is a matter needing attention in our congregations. The art of celebrating with joy is an important part of being a Christian and an individual disciple of Jesus. Joy observed can be attractive and infectious. It can cheer up us sheep in the fold and persuade others to join us, too. How we worship, celebrate communion, greet each other as God's family, are all important elements in being a part of God's flock here. It helps make the lost want to be found and want to return to the security of the fold.

If we take this story seriously, all heaven is on tip-toe breathlessly waiting to see if the one lost will be brought back home again.

We must ask the question: who are the lost of our day? In one sense we are all lost and Jesus has rescued us by going to the cross, coming out of the grave, and returning in Spirit to guide us through this life's wilderness. In that one sense when we gather here, it's the lost celebrating — we are found and rescued by our Savior and are celebrating the joy of it.

In another sense there are many we might consider lost in our day and for whom we must go out and search and bring home again or bring in for the first time.

— Many are lost to addictions such as drugs or alcohol or sexual pleasure or greed and wealth.
— There are those who simply gradually drift away and are now way outside our fold.
— There are those who have given their lives over to immediate gratification and a hedonistic lifestyle.
— There are those we have hurt and/or offended and thus turned off to our church.
— There are those who worked so hard and so long here and because we took advantage of them they left us for less demanding and more peaceful pastures.

Sometimes it's our fault they are lost and in that case we must try even harder and risk even more to help them return. And sometimes we lost some because they simply are bored at the dull way we live out our faith. Real discipleship involves joy, Jesus said. A congregation in celebration ought to be infectious to all who observe or even come near.

Sometimes the lost aren't just those outside the fold either. While here in the fold, we can suffer loss and be in need of rescue. Loss can come in the form of loss of a job or status, loss of spouse or children, loss by divorce or by moving to a different neighborhood and community, and the major one: that of losing to death a loved one.

In all these losses we need to be a sensitive people who seek out each other and bring the quiet joy of companionship and Christian comfort and Christian friendship. It's a ministry to each other that we have as a part of our life in the fold together.

This is also a story about outsiders and insiders. We who are in the church know we are precious to God, our good shepherd. But we don't always realize how precious those still outside the fold are to the shepherd as well. For just one he went back out in the hills and wilderness and searched and searched.

I wonder if the other shepherds didn't say that day that it's not worth the effort just for one. Or maybe they said, as we are often tempted to say, that this lost one was never one of us in the first place!

There are many ways we can communicate that we consider people outsiders: by the language we use in the worship bulletin, by the lack of genuine welcome when they visit us, by the assumption everyone should know how we worship, by a lack of inclusion in our fellowship before and after the service, or by any meaningful action after they visit that fails to say we, too, celebrate their return or first coming to the fold. We insiders must find ways to better celebrate with the good shepherd the lost returning to our fold.

In Ezekiel we have the promise, "As a shepherd looks after his scattered flock when he is with them, so will I look after my sheep. I will rescue them from all the places where they were scattered on a day of clouds and darkness" (Ezekiel 34:12).

God doesn't give up on us. And God takes the initiative and comes out looking for us. Like the loving father after the prodigal son, like this shepherd after the lost sheep, and like the woman who lost her coin and lit a lamp to hunt for it, God searches for us. No one is too far lost or too sinful to invite back or too at fault for being lost. God still tries to bring them (us) back. And the returning of the lost is still cause for great celebration.

In a world of bigness and impersonal numbering of people, in a time when we often feel we are just one among so many, in a culture which often sacrifices the one in order to reach the mass, we have this idea about our God. We count. We are precious to God even with all our dumb straying and stubborn refusal to follow the way we ought to go.

I surely can celebrate this idea of individuality and preciousness by the one who created and continues to operate all the universe. There is joy for celebration for one today. Ezekiel's promise continues as assurance to us and to the lost we seek: "I will search for the lost and bring back the strays. I will bind up the injured and strengthen the weak. I will shepherd the flock with justice" (Ezekiel 34:16).

In this series of messages about the flip side of the parables of Jesus, I wondered what I could come up with on this one which is so familiar and the primary teaching of the story is so clear.

I thought about looking at the sheepfold and the American Express slogan which says it's "everywhere you want to be." We need to be here in the fold in a way others will want to be there, too. Paying attention to possible offenses and anxiety-producing events among our membership is important to cut down on the number who stray and are eventually lost outside the fold.

Then I thought maybe we ought to focus on those who were called the Pharisees or very religious of Jesus' day and how they "muttered" about who he tried to bring into the kingdom. I wondered how many times our dissatisfied muttering has driven away the lost who come close to returning or those inside who just get fed up with all the complaining.

Then it occurred to me that the flip side of this story about the joy of the lost being found is about *those who were never lost at all*. What, after all, are we to do who are already securely in the fold (church)?

We are to support our shepherd's attempts to find the lost. That means to allocate congregational energy and money in a ministry of evangelism and outreach. It means we all need to learn how to witness to our faith and invite others in. It means we must uphold those who are best at seeking the lost wherever they try, in prayer and moral support.

It certainly means we must move beyond expecting our pastor to spread all her/his ministry time caring for us inside and encourage him/her to go out to those not yet enfolded and to teach us how and where to go as well.

When we do all this inside the fold, it will lead to much celebration and joy here and in heaven. How wonderful that will be for the lost and for us, the found, as well.

We need to say this, too. It's only when we take seriously the idea of being lost that our joy at being rescued and rescuing take on their proper importance. Put another way, we must recognize the awfulness of sin to know fully the joy of being saved.

In a time when we rarely talk about sin, this needs to be put on the billboards of life. It's hell to live outside the fold. It can be lonely and bitterly disappointing and sadly dissatisfying. Sin has a way of separating us from God and each other. It has dramatic and drastic implications for our time beyond our grave.

When we realize the gravity of being lost, we begin to realize the joy of being found. It's what Jesus must have had in mind when he told those Pharisees that the shepherd said, "Rejoice with me; I have found my lost sheep" (Luke 15:6b).

What a story about the joy of being found and of finding. It's also about how precious we are to God and what our responsibilities, as those securely within the fold, are for the lost. Ours is not to mutter, but celebrate with joy. We are to erect our signs that say "Linda is O.K." and we are celebrating.

I got them together in their old, old age in Liberia, West Africa. She was Amanda Gardner, called "Mama Ganna," the Bible Woman, and he was called "Old Man" Mopolu, the Evangelist. Both now were beggars, since there was no retirement plan for the aged. As she said goodbye to him for the last time, she wagged her tiny, bony finger in his face and said, "Now, Old Man, don't give up this God business; and when we get to heaven all the people there will greet us with a *big* handclap!" Might that be said of us also!

Love That Just Won't Quit

Luke 15:1-3, 11-32

This parable strikes a sound like fingernails on a blackboard right in the core of my being. I have stood looking down that same road so often praying for a son to return home. I can yet feel the pain and taste the salt of tears on my regretful cheeks as I waited and watched for him to return. Having been the foster father of many young sons, the parable is so real I can barely relate it to you again today.

The youngest of two sons in this parable, probably unmarried and less than twenty years old, asked that he might be given his third of the father's estate early. The very generous father granted it. The young lad went off and squandered it all on what Luke called "wild living." In fact, he really hit bottom and even had to work as a pig feeder, sometimes envying the carob pods he fed the Jew-hated animals.

Then he figured it out — that his father's servants lived better than this — so he decided to go back home and ask his kind father if he could work for him. While he was still down the road, the father ran to him instructing others to bring a robe, a ring, and shoes to put on his feet, symbolizing that this was his son who was home again, a part of the family.

It's one of the greatest short stories ever written. And it didn't stop with the happy celebration of a wayward son returning home. Then came some unpleasant sour grapes.

When the older brother of the returned prodigal saw the celebration, he was incensed. He had stayed home, worked hard for his father, and there hadn't ever been even so much as a young goat given to him for celebration with his friends. Now this rascal of a brother had a big party with a grain-fed calf.

The gracious father again intervened and tried to make it right with both his boys. The lost son and brother had been found and gladness must fill the hearts of the father and both his sons. That's the kind of gracious father he was and that's the kind of sons were his.

By now we know most parables (which means to throw along side of a truth) have only one main teaching. They were told by Jesus to teach something important about his kingdom and about our discipleship. This story has not only a flip side we'll look at in a little bit, but it also has two teachings which must have been meant to be conveyed by Jesus: 1) God loves us sinners no matter how badly we treat God; and, 2) the religious of that day and of our day ought to respond to their brothers and sisters returning home with joy not judgment.

It's a wonderful message we share today because Luke wanted it remembered. When we are tempted to think we have been so bad God surely wouldn't forgive us and receive us back again, this story says: Oh, yes, God would. That's the way God is and that's the main focus of this parable: the loving father who forgives not because his son deserves forgiveness, but because he is his son.

I mentioned earlier that I have also, as a father of many foster teenage sons, watched down that same road. But my inclination, when and if they returned, was to scold them for hurting me or at least to set out some legalistic conditions for their entry back into the family. This father doesn't even wait for his wayward son to arrive. He goes up the road pell-mell with ring and robe and shoes ready to restore his lost son into full membership into the family again. It's the way God works. It's the very nature of our heavenly parent to forgive and do it not because we deserve it, but rather because we are God's baptized sons and daughters and thus family.

I especially like the part where the father makes the first move. I wonder if that isn't exactly what the son knew his loving dad would do. When we gather around the Lord's Table for bread and wine, we are eating the fattened calf with our sisters, brothers, and gracious parent celebrating with all the other returned sinners.

70

Because the Christ went to the cross, you and I can celebrate not only that God takes the initiative and comes after us to receive us home again, but that in the returning we have complete undeserved, unearned, grace-filled forgiveness.

Once when the sheriff, who was a member of the congregation I served, had picked up a wayward son, I drove to the jail to bring him home again. I asked him what he would most like to do now. He responded he just wanted to eat together with the rest of our family around that familiar kitchen table. We do that also when we gather for communion and eat the bread and wine today at this altar.

This is a recklessly extravagant love our God has for us and we gather to celebrate being a part of a family like that. It's a love that just doesn't quit. There aren't any time limits or conditions other than repentance and that doesn't even have to be flawless without imperfect motivation. It's a grace celebration we enjoy and that ought to dictate the nature of the feast. Joy should be obvious and God ought to receive the praise for a love that just won't quit.

Here's something we don't hear very often either: God forgives when people still won't. That's hopeful. It means we ought to reach out to all sorts of people even when their behavior isn't exactly what we would want it to be or of which the community would approve. There is a wideness in God's forgiveness like this beautiful father's. We can count on it even when others are sure we are not any more acceptable to God than we are to others in the congregation.

This is a story about being judgmental. That brings us to the older son. Perhaps this is where many of us find our identification in the story. This fellow should have been so glad his brother had returned, but instead, he let jealousy and envy take over and became consumed with resentment. It's a miserable way to live. But notice the father loved him also and coaxed him to join the banquet as well.

They were two very different sons, both behaving in a way that must have been very disappointing to such a loving father as this. His love wouldn't quit, however. He loved and forgave them both.

71

God does the same for us. Let's celebrate it every time we come together. Let's try our best not to be the self-righteous saints addressed here by Jesus. None of us is that good. We all return home again as imperfect and thus dare not judge another's worth in the family of God.

Now let's turn this parable over and see what we find when we look at it not from its primary focus and teaching, but the flip (other) side.

I'm moved by that older brother's complaint that he had been faithful and served his father well with little, if any, appreciation shown. "My son, you are always with me and everything I have is yours" (Luke 15:31).

Maybe that's not enough, Dad! This father may not have been as perfect as we first thought. He gave wealth to an immature son not yet able to handle it and he neglected to show appreciation to the one who could. Perhaps there ought to be some other celebrating and showing of appreciation.

The scripture says, "... he ran to his son, threw his arms around him and kissed him" (Luke 15:20b). There should have been some hugging and kissing of an older, well-behaved son as well. Let's look around our own families and see if there are not those long-suffering faithful and if we ought not be saying special thanks to them.

We often can take for granted the faithful spouse, the sacrificing mother or father, the dependable son or daughter, the loving, concerned grandparent. To these we ought to tell our love and our appreciation. I wonder if this father had done that adequately in his home over the years.

The flip side of this story also must consider what are the "far countries" which tempt us to stray away like the prodigal son:
— the temptation of adultery outside our marriage;
— the abuse of drugs or alcohol;
— the disregard for precious and nurturing family ties;
— the internet's abundance of pornography;
— the pursuit of wealth for oneself beyond our needs;
— the dark world of racial hatred and prejudice;
— the gradual drifting away from our family.

These may be a bit more subtle than "prostitutes and wild living" but nevertheless they can take us to the far country of our day and culture.

We too, like the prodigal, need to come to our senses. This is no way to live! This is not the rich, fulfilling life available to us. Remember we will be welcomed home again by a love which will not quit. Come on home, for there are brothers and sisters and loving parents who will celebrate your return with you!

We used to have a pony named Tootsie. When we lived outside town we would just tie her to a big truck tire which would allow her to move a little at a time. As Tootsie ate grass she would tug on the halter rope and move on to new and better grass. It was amazing how far she could move in a half day of advancing to better grass. The kids would have to search for her and bring her back home again if they didn't keep a pretty close watch. It was never as if she galloped to a new area, she just slowly ate her way, eventually to a great distance from home.

We can do that same thing, never intentionally moving dramatically away. But rather, slowly getting farther and farther from the disciple's life and teaching. If that's your situation, come on home again. We'll celebrate your return, too.

Because this story talks of a father giving his sons their inheritance, I can't resist saying something about the Christian stewardship involved in how we handle this matter of inheritance in our own lives.

We happen to live in a society and country which is sophisticated in its laws about inheritance. And there are many wonderful things we can arrange ahead of time for the inheritance we plan for others. It may not always be the case that passing on everything we have accumulated to our children is the best way to dispose of it. Like the loving father and younger son in our story, we may not be making life better for them as we had hoped.

There are some steps we can take now to help ensure that the inheritance we pass on will be a blessing and not just "wild living" in the far country. In order to do this we must have our up-to-date will in place. We can even decide how we would like our funeral to be a witness to our faith. It's the Christian thing to do, to have this all thought out ahead of time.

Some suggestions for the Christian disposition of our estate to be included in our will could be:

1. Have an up-to-date will.
2. Tithe the estate to your church with as few strings attached as possible.
3. Consider a major gift to one or two of your church's institutions like a theological seminary, home for the elderly, college, or treatment center for children.
4. Consider an amount in your will to go to Global Mission or world hunger.
5. Most national church bodies have a foundation to which you can designate some of your estate. This supports ministries abroad and at home.
6. Don't forget that it's possible to participate in what is called a guaranteed life annuity. This means you can give the money now like the loving father in the parable. In addition you can receive the income off the money for your use and can also take a deduction off your income tax over the next several years.

A Christian lawyer who understands the financial stewardship of us disciples can help you with this financial planning. The church also has specialists in the field available to you. I'll be glad to put you in touch with these people because I believe it's what that loving father should have done and what we ought to do also. This does seem pretty far from why Jesus told the story in the first place, but very close to what we in America with so much wealth ought to consider.

It's my prayer that this day and this sermon on the parable will be memorable for all of us as we consider being good stewards of our estates, good parents to our children, good people staying out of the far country, good church members who celebrate the return of some who have strayed, and good daughters and sons of God, confident we can come home and be loved again.

I've stood out there on that same road watching for that same prodigal — he did return and how we rejoiced. For a son of ours "... was dead and is alive again; he was lost and is found" (Luke 15:32b).

Dog-Licked Sores
And Linen Underwear

Luke 16:19-31

I wonder if there has ever been a study of how the kind of underwear we wear affects our behavior. This wealthy man named Dives in our parable for today wore underwear of fine linen, according to Luke. In fact, he said that the man was so wealthy that he "... lived in luxury every day" (Luke 16:19b). Purple was the color of royal robes and "fine linen" described the very best undergarments. There is nothing wrong with his fine underwear except that he thought everyone wore it. Listen to this wonderfully told story so that not a sentence is wasted.

[1]*There was this very wealthy man who lived luxuriously, not a couple days a week, but all the time. In contrast, there was a cripple covered with sores who begged at his gate. His name was Lazarus, which means "God is my help." It's a good thing God was his help because Dives didn't even seem to notice this wretched man who was so weak he couldn't keep the dogs from licking his open sores. The man had wasted there day after day to get the hunks of bread used by the rich to wipe their hands in place of napkins. Dives walked by in his purple, royal robe and linen underwear without seeing the pitiful scene.

Then the two died and everything is reversed. The one with the sores of poverty went straight to heaven and the one with the fine underwear went straight to hell! Typical of the aloof and wealthy, Dives thought Lazarus should come and help him. But no — there was a big gulf between the two so that it was not possible!

Then Dives got serious and asked Abraham to send someone to warn his five brothers about how it is in eternity for the linen undergarment wearers. But Abraham said simply that if they hadn't listened to Moses and the prophets they probably wouldn't "be convinced even if someone rises from the dead" (Luke 16:31b).

A little later we'll look at the flip side of this marvelous story and what the motivations are for our good works, the lesson about witnessing to our own family members, and something about heaven and hell. None of which will have anything to do with the kind of underwear we put on.

2)Now let's turn to the more traditional approach to this parable. It tells us a lot about our God. It says loud and clear that what God delights in is our having compassion on others.

Luke had written Jesus' words earlier, "What is highly valued among people is detestable in God's sight" (Luke 16:15b). In other words, God hasn't ordered it that some be so rich and live so luxuriously and others like Lazarus have such a pitiful existence. I'm certain God also loves us all alike: the wealthy, the poor, the misfit, the extrovert, the manipulator, the dependent, the con man, and the straight arrow.

There are situations which God must permit to exist in order to be a dependable God. That doesn't mean God wants them to be like that. This beggar with the dogs and sores was one of them. Our God is a loving one who wants the very best for us. And one who just might be a bit reluctant to receive us into heaven in our silk underwear when all around us there are those who can afford none at all.

I've heard misguided preaching, especially in Brazil and Chile, South America, and from German Lutheran pulpits which claimed that the poor's worldly situation was bad but that it was God's will. However, they would be rewarded in heaven for putting up with their worldly situation.

They may have wrongly interpreted this parable or maybe they were wearing the fine linen underwear themselves. In any case, it's just not true. God wants our circumstances to be the best possible and when they are, wants us to help those whose are not.

3)This story also tells us about ourselves. One of the curses of wealth happens when we begin to overlook those who don't have it, like Dives did Lazarus. In his fine robes and linen underwear he didn't see those in need around him. He might even become so divorced from the real earthly world that he assumed everyone could live, eat, and dress as he did.

We Americans can be like that. If we have not traveled to other countries we assume everyone has it as good as we do. And when the occasional television news program shows abject poverty which is a part of so much of the world, we are stunned to see it. Or we get such a steady diet of those pictures of famine and disease we become immune to their pull on our heart.

Isaiah 58:7 points out that the kind of fasting God wants of us is "... to share your food with the hungry and to provide the poor wanderers with shelter — when you see the naked, to cloth them, and not to turn away from your own flesh and blood."

During one of my visits with our foster daughter, now living in Montevideo, Uruguay, she wanted to show me the cathedral where the Pope had recently celebrated mass. When we got to the massive main wooden doors there was a homeless woman lying there in rags and throwing up. Our daughter, Beatriz, bent over to see if she could help. Her husband, Antonio, said the woman was there every day and that we should step over her and go in to see the fabulous church. Beatriz refused and stated: "First we help this woman, then we'll see the beauty of the cathedral."

That day I saw the beauty of compassion far beyond that of a grand cathedral. Our tendency is to not even notice. Jesus tells us to do differently. We must see and help on God's behalf.

[4]My guess is that Luke recorded this story for us because he thought that after Jesus' crucifixion and Easter resurrection and the return in the Spirit at Pentecost, this would explain why the religious of his day refused to be converted even though Easter had taken place and there were many witnesses to it. Jesus says, "... if they do not listen to Moses and the Prophets, they will not be convinced even if someone rises from the dead" (Luke 16:31b). And, of course, that's exactly what he did and many were not convinced either.

I suspect Luke wanted to hold up Jesus' teaching here that there would be a reversal of roles in the afterlife, too. He probably took delight in that almost vindictive idea that the rich would be poor and the poor rich. No more fine linen underwear for old Dives and no less than the angels carried poor Lazarus right to the side of Father Abraham.

While it may have been the reason Luke recorded this parable for us, I doubt it's what Jesus wanted to teach from it. He wanted us to see the needy in our midst and for his sake help them. He wanted us to be aware of the dangers of wealth addiction which could dull our sensitivity to those who have so much less.

5)Now let's look for a fresh and new approach to an old, old story. If we turn this parable upside down and look at its other side, *we learn a little about the afterlife, something about witnessing to our family members, and a new motivation after the crucifixion to have compassion for those less fortunate than us.*

It's wrong to consider this hypothetical teaching story as a lesson on the mechanics of eternal life. But we can say a little about how we see those "states of being" now in the twenty-first century. I like the contemporary definition of heaven as being with God and as hell as being left alone by our own choice.

The rest of the Bible gives us very little to go on other than to say it won't be the same for everyone beyond the grave. Most of us reject the old idea of hell as torment or a heaven of gold pavement and pearly gates. But we know Jesus died on a cross so we might know God's forgiveness and love for us, and Jesus came out of the grave so that we need not worry about our grave either. We might add it's what God did that makes this possible and not what we do here on earth that makes us deserving of our reward.

The way we help others, I believe, also demonstrates what heaven might be like. An evangelist, Tom Skinner, told us at a Florida conference: "God's intention is that the church shall establish itself in an alien territory so people can see what heaven is like. We pray it in the Lord's Prayer. It's like the English came to Africa and Africans could see what living in England is like." So we have compassion on the poor at our door and others can taste a little heaven.

Remember Jesus told this story before he had died for us. Back then, one's heaven or hell was completely dependent on how one lived life here. Today, after the cross of Calvary we have a much better and happier motivation for noticing those in need and helping them.

If we really believe God's son has died a cruel death for our forgiveness and that God's son came out of the grave so we might also, then we have compassion on others because of all God has done for us. We love others because God first loved us. We feel sorry for others because God shows sorrow for us — not in order to have heaven with Abraham, but in order to respond properly to the accomplished fact we have heaven given to us as undeserving as we are.

Martin Luther claimed we don't do good deeds to be saved, but if we are saved we just can't help ourselves but to do them. And I'd add — that's whether we can afford linen underwear or not!

Did you notice that there was some compassion expressed by Dives? He said to Abraham, "... send Lazarus to my father's house, for I have five brothers. Let him warn them, so that they will not also came to this place of torment" (Luke 16:27-28).

While it certainly wasn't in the original story to encourage us to speak to our family members about the faith, I don't think it dishonest to use it that way. Statistics in the U.S. reveal that each one of us hearing this sermon knows six to eight unchurched people who live near enough to this church to be active members. Many of these are members of our own family.

I'm reminded by the parable that it's a good thing and right that we have heart-to-heart talks to them about our faith. We can do this in a non-judgmental, loving, concerned way that neither offends nor turns them off to Christ and the church. It's often just a matter of inviting them to come to worship with you. It might mean telling them about your relationship to God and God's people and then listening for them to share theirs. By all means it does not mean to threaten with punishment or hell.

In an effective witness to people you know and care about (i.e., family members) there ought to be three stories shared: your story, their story, and God's story. When those intersect, the Spirit of God can be most effective.

In this parable, Abraham said he doubted if someone rose from the dead it would convince those five brothers. But in our case, now that one did rise from the dead, it's often a matter of inviting. If this parable can get us to do this, it certainly will have been worth Jesus' time in telling it and Luke's effort in writing it down.

[6]I'll be interested in hearing what all of you think we should do as individual Christians and as a congregation of compassionate disciples of Jesus because we have considered this parable. We ought to pray for a new sensitivity to the plight of the poor and for the insight of how best to help them. We ought to be warned of getting calloused to need which may be all around us.

We ought to resolve to thank God for our undeserved eternity by inviting those most apt to accept our witness to God's grace. And if you think of a person right now who could use your help, why not try even yet today?

[7]Our Uruguayan daughter Beatriz's words sound clearly in my ears yet today: "First we'll help the woman, then we'll see the cathedral."

It would be an interesting study to see if the type of underwear we wear affects our behavior. I suspect it does. I suspect it affected rich Dives and poor Lazarus also. Nevertheless, wear what we like or nothing at all — we are challenged to take notice and do *something* about the Lazarus at our door.

---

*The numbers in this sermon correspond to the steps outlined in the introduction to this book for preaching on a parable.

Going Home Justified

Luke 18:9-14

In the beautiful, romantic, walled town of Rothenburg ob der Tauber in Germany, there is a strange museum called Kriminal-museum. There you can find on display a number of "shame masks" used mostly by Austrians in the seventeenth and eighteenth centuries.

Constructed out of metal and locked on the offender's head, the masks are to be worn in public as punishment for a certain length of time. One, shaped like a pig's snout, was worn by someone being punished for acting like a pig. Another has metal chicken feathers on it for someone without sexual restraint. One more had a big nose for a person who was always sticking his/her nose in other people's business.

The mask which probably fits the parable we consider today was one with a mammoth tongue, big ears, and big glasses — for that person who saw everything and talked way too much!

Jesus told this story of two people going to pray in the temple (probably at the prescribed time for prayer, either 9:00 a.m. or 3:00 p.m.). The story was told to "... some who were confident of their own righteousness and looked down on everyone else" (Luke 18:9). These worshipers could use one of those Austrian shame masks, especially the first to pray might be a good candidate for one. Jesus said this Pharisee "... prayed about himself: 'God, I thank you that I am not like other men — robbers, evildoers, adulterers — or even like this tax collector' " (Luke 18:11). His prayer sounds like a popular song of some years ago: "O Lord, it's hard to be humble when you're perfect in every way."

In contrast to the Pharisee, Jesus said a tax collector (who faced great temptation to cheat his fellow Jews in collecting taxes from them) "... stood at a distance. He would not even look up to heaven, but beat his breast and said, 'God, have mercy on me, a sinner'" (Luke 18:13).

This contrast is certainly extreme to make the main point. We must not count on our own goodness to put us right with God and we must guard against looking down on other people. It also has a lot to say about how we ought to pray. The flip side will be an interesting exploration of how we live together after we go home justified. But that comes a little later.

It's not difficult to be in the sandals of that Pharisee, especially we who come to worship and serve in many ways in the church's ministry. We can often begin to think we are better than those who rarely darken the church doors and then only as a spectator who contributes almost nothing to the work of the church. It's easy to think "Look at me, Jesus, I'm trying hard. I tithe and fill out the pledge card. I serve on a committee. I sing the hymns even when they are strange to me. I'm not like those others." Perhaps we all ought to have one of those masks out of the Rothenburg Kriminalmuseum to wear over our proud heads!

On the way to Rothenburg we drove our little rental car on the German autobahn. The left lane is for passing. There is a sort of hierarchy on that raceway. The BMW and Mercedes drivers come up behind you no matter how fast you are going, flash the lights, and come right up to the bumper until you move over. It felt to me as though they were arrogant. We can be arrogant as church members as well.

Saint Paul seemed to understand this much better. He let us know in very clear terms that it wasn't our own good works which could put us right with God. It was, rather, what God has done in the person of our Savior, the Christ. Listen: "For all have sinned and fall short of the glory of God, and are justified freely by God's grace through the redemption that came by Jesus Christ" (Romans 3:23-24).

So, you see, counting on our own good works and holiness just won't do it. This fellow who prayed so self-righteously in the temple that day was a good temple member and did many good things there. In fact, according to the story, he did much more than the Jewish law required of a religious person. Instead of once a week, he fasted twice a week. Instead of tithing just on what was required he tithed on *all* he received.

We would love to have him as a member here, unless he was one of those arrogant members who thought they were better than everyone else, unless he was one of those legalistic members who saw religion as stern and judgmental and was always criticizing everyone else.

This fellow's shortcoming was not that he didn't do nice and good and admirable things, it's just that he did them all for the wrong reasons. The worst sort of sin is self-righteousness. And he was counting on credit for all that religious practice to justify him with God.

Give the man one of those "shame masks" and require him to wear it in the entryway to our sanctuary to remind us you just can't be good enough to earn favor with God. God has already done that in offering Jesus, his only son, on the cross as a sacrifice for our sins and as a way to make it all right with our God. That's the way our God is: full of grace and ready to make things all right between us and our creator, even though we don't deserve it at all!

While self-confidence that we are so good that God just has to love us is a big temptation, I believe our natural temptation to look down on others is an even stronger temptation. There seems to be something in our human nature that wants us to put down other people which, in our sinfulness, makes us feel more superior.

This strong tendency causes wars, strife between neighbors, discontent among employees, discord in marriages, and hatred between races, nationalities, and ethnic groups. It is a powerful, demonic part of our human nature and we must guard against it. Naming this bigotry and holding it up to the light so all can see, and gently admonishing others to refrain from it, will help.

One of the beautiful things discipleship and the New Testament teach us about life is to appreciate all kinds and sorts of people as unique and loved by the creator. It says we all have our rich contribution to the cultural mix and to the well-being of the world-wide family. One of us is better at one thing and another at something else. It makes for a pluralistic, global family which is not to be looked down upon but celebrated and appreciated.

We must now turn to the second pray-er in the temple that day. His prayer was so humble and perhaps so desperate as well: "God, have mercy on me, a sinner" (Luke 18:13b). This fellow knew he could find many worse than himself with whom to compare his life and thus feel superior. Luke wrote the story after Jesus had died on the cross and after he had modeled the godly life as a human being. When we compare our life to his model and his teaching, all we can say is the same as the tax collector, "God, have mercy on me, a sinner."

What a contrast in how we ought to pray. And what a contrast in how we ought to come to worship — not proud of all we have done here, but humble in the knowledge of all we could have done.

This business of humility is something we have nearly forgotten in our country and culture. In our rush to not be trampled on we have gone overboard in claiming we should assert ourselves, we should demand our rights, we must stake out our turf. We have taught our youth to love self, to celebrate our worth, and so forth. All this, it seems to me, was needed in order to move them away from being what we call "wimps."

It certainly was helpful to people long-oppressed who needed some empowerment as a remedy for their oppression. But it has developed into a culture which idolizes power and self-worth to the exclusion of and almost embarrassment about humbleness. It has produced a self-centered, egotistical people always demanding more for themselves, certain they are better than everyone else.

This tax collector praying had it right. He knew, or would know, the truth of Jesus' teaching: "Blessed are the meek for they will inherit the earth" (Matthew 5:5). He simply prayed, "God, have mercy on me, a sinner." Jesus then said, "... he who humbles himself will be exalted" (Luke 18:14b).

We often present a laundry list of "give-me's" when we pray. God, I want this. God, please do that. Even in our Lutheran worship in this country we have all but lost the meaningful element of confession and absolution. Yet it is one example of the strong equipment we Christians have to offer the rest of the world. If we fail to recognize sin and its effects on our lives, we may not feel the need to ask for mercy. But that is our big loss.

For your next prayer consider an age-old formula used by many early church fathers and mothers — ACTS:

Adoration: Begin by praising our God.

Confession: Tell God your behavior and thoughts which have been wrong and are heavy on your conscience.

Thanksgiving: Thank God for the many blessings you enjoy each day.

Supplication: Ask God to help you do, behave, and believe the way you ought as one of Jesus' followers.

Try not just talking to God — although that is a good thing to do. Try quietly *listening* to God. Prayer ought to be a two-way dialogue when God speaks to us as well.

Notice the Pharisee in the parable had a lot to say to God. Stuff God already knew, by the way. Notice the tax collector simply asked for mercy. And, according to Luke, Jesus said it was this simple, humble prayer which worked: "I tell you that this man, rather than the other, went home justified before God" (Luke 18:14). Some have defined our praying as time when we purposely make God's will for us our desire.

Try having a sacred, quiet place where you can each day be listening for God's will in your life. That's a far cry from this arrogant Pharisee church pillar's reporting all the good things he had done, even looking down on another of God's own people for whom his son would die on Jerusalem's cross. No person who hates another can really pray.

That tax collector's humility reminds me of an Iowa farmer I heard about during the farm crisis in the early '80s when I was a parish pastor in Des Moines. He bought a new John Deere tractor but asked that it be delivered at night so he could put the old tractor's decals on it so it would not appear new. He didn't want to "lord it over" his Iowa neighbors who were struggling to survive financially.

The flip side of this parable, probably not told for this purpose, but worth mentioning for our edification, now is twofold: Since the crucifixion, *both kinds of prayers are justified; and how is it that those of us going home justified now live together?*

Here is a radical thought about God. Both of these men have the benefit of God's grace. We often read the story and think this Pharisee will go straight to hell. Not so, since God worked the atonement on the cross. Our sins are forgiven, even those of the Pharisee!

So if this sermon about the pride of a good church member has troubled you (and I hope it has), you too can celebrate that God knew we would be the way we are and in God's graceful way forgave us. How's that for the back side of a parable? Some complain that the church is full of Pharisees and hypocrites. It is, and it's a good place for us to be. For here we, too, can be justified.

It's also worth thinking about how we live with each other justified. According to Luke, Jesus said, "This man ... went home justified before God" (Luke 18:14). Since that's the situation, we have to ask if home was any different that week? Certainly for justified people, there ought to be a wideness in our mercy shown to each other. We are sinners and forgiven by God, so we forgive the other imperfect people we live with.

It's a radical mercy and forgiveness we offer each other as God offers us. The honor of being "justified before God" can and ought to be a place of undeserved love for each other. It ought to be a place of prayer and humility rather than arrogant demands to be treated fairly.

Our homes ought to celebrate our differences and never demonstrate belittling another human being. A good dose of humility probably would help the atmosphere in our homes and our relationships with each other.

So on the flip side of this story of a humble and an arrogant pray-er, there is this surprise: that all kinds of sinners are forgiven and that because we are forgiven and have been given undeserved mercy, we ought to change not only how we pray but how we live with each other!

Add to this an excellent lesson in how to pray, our need for humility, the sin of putting down others, and the primary side of the story that we must be careful about pride in our practice of religion, and you have quite a parable.

There was another item in that Kriminalmuseum. It was a giant, heavy rosary carved out of wood. When members fell asleep during the sermon or failed to attend worship, it was placed around their neck for punishment. I hope none of you qualify for wearing it during this sermon!

I still think if I could just get back to that Rothenburg museum, pick up some of those shame masks, and be the first to wear one in the entryway, we'd all know the truth: "For everyone who exalts himself will be humbled, and he who humbles himself will be exalted" (Luke 18:14b).